STEADY IN THE STORM

A STOIC TOOLKIT FOR HARD TIMES, PERSONAL GROWTH, AND INNER PEACE

EMILY BRIARS

Steady in the Storm

In memory of my late husband,
whose great influence will remain with me always, and to my grandma, whose strength, self-discipline, and inner calm are the foundation to my living a good life, despite its difficulties, and the portal to the world of Stoicism.

Thank you both for being the inspiration for my book.

CONTENTS

Preface: Steadfast in the Storm vii
Introduction xi

1. The Stoic Resilience Toolkit 1
2. The Stoic's Guide to Thriving in the Modern Workplace 17
3. Navigating Friendships 29
4. Relative Chaos 47
5. Rebuilding After a Breakup 67
6. Life After Loss 79
7. Embracing Life by Facing Death 91
8. Anchored in Chaos 100

Author's Note 105
About the Author 109
Bibliography 111

PREFACE: STEADFAST IN THE STORM

"Be like the rock that the waves keep crashing over. It stands unmoved, and the raging of the sea falls still around it."

— MARCUS AURELIUS, MEDITATIONS

My introduction to Stoicism came, not from books, but from my grandma, whose intuitive wisdom mirrored the Stoic teachings. Though she never studied philosophy formally, she embodied resilience and acceptance, values that later became a guiding force in my life. Widowed at an early age, she was left to raise four children with little money and few options. Rather than succumb to bitterness or despair, she rolled up her sleeves, taking on three jobs to keep her family afloat.

Her mantra was simple: "It is, and that's an end of it. Now, what will you do?" At first glance, her words might seem blunt, even harsh. But they carried a profound truth. First, accept reality without resistance or denial. Then, remind yourself that action is always within your control, no matter how dire the circumstances. Together, these words encapsulate the Stoic mindset: acknowledge what you cannot change and channel your energy into what you can.

Her wisdom resurfaced two months after the worst day of my life. Overwhelmed by grief, I found myself stuck in traffic in a London taxi on a cold, rainy January night. The cabbie, who must have been curious about my sombre demeanour, asked me about my life. Exhausted, I answered plainly. After listening, he glanced at me in the rear-view mirror and said, "Blimey, how sad. I don't know how you've kept going."

I managed a faint smile and replied, "My grandma. She's the reason I'm still standing." Intrigued, he asked me to explain. I shared her mantra, and his face lit up, as though hearing a piece of long-lost wisdom. That moment made me reflect—not on how hard or sad my life seemed to others, but on how her words had always guided me to keep moving forward. Sharing her wisdom reminded me that, even in my darkest moment, I still had the power to take the first step toward healing. That conversation marked the beginning of a new chapter for me.

Her mantra serves as a reminder to me that Stoicism isn't an abstract intellectual exercise but a living, breathing practice. It provides a practical guide to facing challenges with resilience and rediscovering joy in the present moment. Stoicism teaches us to weather life's tempests and live with purpose, joy, and balance by focusing on what truly matters: relationships, personal growth, and integrity. By letting go of what we can't control and embracing what we can, Stoicism anchors us to our values and priorities. It reveals meaning not only in moments of triumph but in the quiet, everyday experiences that shape our lives.

We all face struggles which differ in form and magnitude. My experiences may not mirror your own, and so this is not an autobiography, nor is it limited to the lessons of my own experiences. Instead, it is a reflection of what I believe: that no matter the nature of our hardships, Stoicism offers a universal guide to navigating them. The scenarios chosen in this book are ones many of us have likely encountered in one form or another, offering insights that are universally relatable and practical.

Like the rock Marcus Aurelius describes, standing firm as the waves crash over it, Stoicism teaches us to stay steady in life's storms. In that steadiness, you find something deeper: quiet strength, clarity, and the rediscovery of joy.

This book won't erase hardship—but it will redefine how you see it. Struggle can sharpen you. Obstacles can instruct you. Resilience can become who you are. You can't always control life, but you can control how you navigate it.

INTRODUCTION

A STOIC BLUEPRINT- TIMELESS WISDOM FOR MODERN LIFE

What if, instead of just reacting to life, you could feel *truly* in control—choosing how you think, feel, and respond to pressure, unpredictability, and challenges?

Too often, we wait—for circumstances to change, for others to act differently, or for life to get easier. But real power comes when we stop waiting and start engaging with life on our own terms. Instead of being ruled by what's outside our control, we shift our focus to what we *can* control—our mindset, our actions, our responses. That shift changes everything.

This mindset has guided some of history's greatest minds through chaos, uncertainty, and hardship—helping them rise above it. Imagine moving through life with that same steadiness, no matter what comes your way. No longer weighed down by "what ifs" or regret, we shift our perspective and ask: *What now?*

Instead of feeling powerless, we recognize our ability to shape our choices. No longer passive, we take control where it matters most—becoming architects of our actions. We define who we want to be, and then we act accordingly.

As Epictetus put it, "First, say to yourself what you would be, and then do what you have to do."

His words remind us that change begins with intention—by deciding who we want to be and following through with action.

Stoicism is a philosophy that teaches resilience, self-discipline, and the pursuit of virtue by focusing on what we can control and accepting what we cannot. It encourages maintaining inner peace amidst life's challenges through wisdom, courage, justice, and temperance.

The wisdom of Stoicism is timeless, and its brilliance lies in its practical application—it doesn't change the external world, but it fundamentally transforms how we engage with it, not through a radical overhaul, but through small, deliberate steps.

A Timeless Philosophy for a Changing World

For over two millennia, Stoicism has provided a framework for resilience, wisdom, and clarity—first in the streets of ancient Athens, then in the courts of Rome, and now, in the challenges of modern life.

Founded by Zeno of Citium around 300 BCE, and later refined by Epictetus, Seneca, and Marcus Aurelius, Stoicism has endured because it was not just theorized but lived (Long, 2002). Though rooted in the ancient world, its principles remain as relevant today as they were in the bustling markets of Athens or the halls of Roman power.

Forged in Adversity—A Philosophy Tested by Life

- Zeno of Citium lost everything in a shipwreck—but instead of despairing, he built a philosophy that turned hardship into strength (Diogenes Laërtius, 1925).
- Marcus Aurelius, a Roman Emperor navigating war and political turmoil, relied on Stoicism to cultivate inner peace and resilience. His personal reflections, now known as *Meditations*, remain one of the greatest texts on self-mastery (Aurelius, trans. 2006).

If Stoicism could guide great minds through war and exiles through hardship, it can certainly help us navigate the complexities of modern life.

Ancient Principles, Modern Challenges

The world has changed in ways the ancient Stoics could never have imagined, yet the human experience remains the same.

We may not face shipwrecks or political conspiracies, but we grapple with:

- Workplace pressure and career uncertainty
- Relationship conflicts and emotional struggles
- The relentless noise of a hyperconnected world

While technology and society evolve, the core struggles of uncertainty, fear, loss, and ambition remain unchanged. And that is why Stoicism endures.

But understanding its origins is just the first step. To truly benefit from Stoicism, we need to see how its core principles fit together—how they form a structured philosophy that shapes our mindset, decisions, and actions.

So, how does Stoic thought translate into daily life? How do its key ideas—virtue, control, perception, and resilience—interconnect to create a practical framework for living well?

The Four Layers of Stoic Practice

Stoicism is not just a set of abstract ideas—it is a practical framework for living with resilience, wisdom, and purpose. At first glance, its concepts—virtue, control, fate, and discipline—might seem separate, but they all work together toward a single goal: *Eudaimonia*, a life of deep well-being and fulfilment (Hadot, 1995).

To make Stoicism structured and applicable, we can break it down into four interconnected layers:

1. **Living in Accord with Nature** – The guiding principle.
2. **The Four Cardinal Virtues** – The ethical foundation.
3. **The Triangle of Happiness** – A practical framework.
4. **The Nine Core Principles** – The tools for daily discipline.

Each layer builds upon the one before it. Without the first, the rest cannot stand. When all four align, Stoicism becomes more than a philosophical study—it becomes a way of thinking, acting, and responding to life's challenges with clarity and resilience.

Layer 1: Living in Accord with Nature – The Underlying Principle

At the core of Stoicism is a simple but profound idea: to live well, we must align ourselves with reality, not resist it (Sellars, 2006).

This does not mean passively accepting everything that happens. Instead, it means:

- **Accepting change** – Life is constantly shifting. Resisting it leads to frustration.
- **Understanding our role** – We are social beings, meant to contribute to the world around us.
- **Acting with reason** – Unlike other creatures, we have the ability to think rationally. Using this wisely is what sets us apart.

When we fight reality, we suffer. When we work with it, we thrive. This is why the Stoics saw living in accord with nature as the foundation of everything else.

Layer 2: The Four Cardinal Virtues – The Ethical Foundation

If Living in Accord with Nature is the underlying principle, virtue is how we put it into action. The Stoics defined four core virtues that guide every decision and action (Robertson, 2019):

1. **Wisdom** – The ability to think clearly, make rational choices, and seek truth.
2. **Courage** – Facing difficulty without fear and acting with integrity.
3. **Justice** – Treating others fairly and contributing to the greater good.
4. **Temperance** – Exercising self-discipline and avoiding excess.

The Moral Compass Analogy

"If a man knows not to which port he sails, no wind is favourable."
—Seneca (Seneca, trans. 1997)

These virtues function as a moral compass, guiding our thoughts, actions, and decisions. Just as a compass keeps a traveller on the right path, these four virtues keep us aligned with reason and integrity, helping us navigate challenges with clarity and purpose.

Without a compass, a traveller is lost. Without virtue, we drift aimlessly, reacting to life rather than directing it. Therefore, the Four Cardinal Virtues are the ethical bedrock of Stoicism.

This Stoic approach to life has influenced modern therapeutic practices such as Cognitive Behavioural Therapy (CBT) and Rational Emotive Behaviour Therapy (REBT) (Ellis, 1962; Beck, 1976). By reframing our thoughts, focusing on what is within our control, and taking purposeful action, we build resilience, reduce anxiety, and lead more fulfilling lives.

Layer 3: The Triangle of Happiness – The Applied Framework

While the Four Cardinal Virtues serve as our moral compass, we also need a practical structure for applying Stoicism to daily life. That's where the *Triangle of Happiness* comes in.

This framework consists of three interdependent elements:

1. **Virtue** – The ethical foundation of a meaningful life. Living with wisdom, courage, justice, and temperance leads to inner fulfilment.
2. **Control** – Recognizing what we can and cannot control reduces stress and frees us from unnecessary worry.
3. **Action** – Taking deliberate steps aligned with our values ensures we live with intention rather than passivity.

Apatheia: Inner Stability in a Chaotic World

At the heart of this framework is *Apatheia*, a term often misunderstood. It does not mean being emotionless or indifferent. Instead, it refers to a state of inner calm, clarity, and freedom from destructive emotions (Long, 2002).

The Stoics believed that true strength comes from self-discipline, mastering our impulses, and focusing only on what we can control. *Apatheia* is not about suppressing emotions, but about responding to life with reason rather than being ruled by passions.

How Apatheia Connects to the Triangle of Happiness

- **Virtue** keeps us anchored in ethical decision-making.
- **Control** helps us detach from unnecessary worry and focus only on what matters.
- **Action** ensures we respond deliberately rather than impulsively.

When all three are in place, we develop *Apatheia*—an unshakable sense of calm and focus, even in difficult situations.

Aurelius summed it up perfectly. “You have power over your mind—not outside events. Realize this, and you will find strength” (Marcus Aurelius, trans. 2006).

By cultivating *Apatheia*, we gain freedom from suffering caused by external events, allowing us to live with clarity, resilience, and inner peace.

Layer 4: The Nine Core Principles – The Tools for Everyday Life

The Nine Core Stoic Principles are the practical habits that reinforce Stoicism in real-world situations. They align with the Four Virtues and the Triangle of Happiness, helping us apply Stoicism to everyday challenges.

Each principle serves as a mental discipline, shaping the way we think, act, and respond. Together, they strengthen self-discipline, resilience, and clarity, allowing us to focus on what truly matters.

Unlike a strict doctrine, these principles are not rigid rules but recurring ideas woven throughout Stoic writings. Marcus Aurelius, Epictetus, and Seneca never laid them out in a numbered format, yet these core themes consistently appear in their teachings (Long, 2002; Sellars, 2006).

This list serves as a practical framework—a set of mental habits designed to help us navigate difficulties, make better decisions, and cultivate inner strength. The goal is not just to understand Stoicism, but to live it.

If you are interested in connecting these ideas to *Meditations*, a reference guide at the end of this book links the Nine Core Stoic Principles to key passages from Marcus Aurelius' writings.

1. The Dichotomy of Control: Focus on What You Can Influence

At the heart of Stoicism is a simple but transformative idea (Epictetus, trans. 2008):

- Some things are within our control—our thoughts, actions, and decisions.
- Other things are not—external events, other people's opinions, and unexpected setbacks.

Most frustration comes from fighting what we can't change. A long queue, bad weather, someone else's attitude—these things are beyond our control.

Instead of wasting energy, the Stoic asks:

- What is within my control right now?
- How can I respond with wisdom and discipline?

By mastering this mindset, we free ourselves from unnecessary suffering.

2. Virtue is the Highest Good

Success isn't measured by wealth, status, or recognition, but by the kind of person we become.

In Stoicism, virtue—living with wisdom, courage, justice, and temperance—is the only true measure of a life well lived (Robertson, 2019).

That doesn't mean Stoics dismissed health, wealth, or success. They saw these as "preferred indifferents"—things that can make life easier, but don't define its value (Sellars, 2006). Money can provide security, but it can't create meaning. Good health is a gift, but it doesn't guarantee happiness.

Hardship, illness, or failure—what Stoics called "dispreferred indifferents"—may be unpleasant, but they are not inherently bad (Long, 2002). A wealthy person can be miserable, while someone facing adversity can still live with purpose and strength.

The Stoics remind us that fulfilment doesn't come from what we have, but from how we live. Before making a decision, the Stoic asks:

- Am I doing this because it's right or because I want approval?
- Am I measuring success by my values or by someone else's standards?

Happiness is not found in possessions or circumstances—it's

found in the way we think, act, and respond to life and acting with integrity.

3. Memento Mori: Remember the Impermanence of Life

Reflecting on mortality doesn't make life morbid—it makes it meaningful (Hadot, 1995).

Nothing is guaranteed. We don't know how much time we have. The Stoics used this reality to focus on what truly matters:

- The conversation we've been avoiding.
- The risks we've been too hesitant to take.

Instead of waiting, the Stoic lives deliberately—today, not someday.

4. *Amor Fati*: Love and Accept Fate

Life doesn't always go as planned. The Stoics believed that instead of resisting challenges, we should embrace them.

Marcus Aurelius wrote, "What stands in the way becomes the way" (Aurelius, trans. 2006).

- What if this challenge isn't happening *against* me, but *for* me?
- What can I learn from this?

When we accept what happens and use it as fuel, we turn obstacles into opportunities.

5. Negative Visualisation: Prepare for Challenges Before They Happen

The Stoics practiced *Premeditatio Malorum*—imagining what could go wrong, not to dwell on it, but to be mentally prepared (Robertson, 2019).

Before a big event, it helps to ask:

- What's the worst that could happen?
- How would I handle it?

When we expect setbacks, we build resilience.

6. The View from Above: Gain Perspective

Marcus Aurelius often imagined looking down on life from above, seeing the bigger picture (Aurelius, trans. 2006).

From a higher perspective, problems that feel overwhelming shrink into their proper size.

- Will this matter in a week? A year? Five years?

Most problems are temporary—and many are not worth the stress we give them.

7. Sympatheia: Recognise Our Shared Humanity

Stoicism isn't just about personal resilience—it's also about how we relate to others. We are all connected, and justice, compassion, and community matter (Hadot, 1995).

It's easy to get frustrated with people, but the Stoics remind us to take a step back.

- Everyone we meet is facing their own struggles.
- They have fears, hopes, and imperfections—just like us.

When we recognise this, we become:

- More patient
- Less reactive
- More focused on what really matters

Justice and compassion are as central to Stoicism as discipline and logic.

8. Discipline & Temperance: Master Desires and Emotions

True strength isn't about overpowering others—it's about mastering ourselves (Sellars, 2006).

The more control we have over our impulses, the more control we have over our lives.

In moments of anger, frustration, or temptation, the Stoic pauses and asks:

- Am I making this decision based on impulse, or reason?

Small moments of self-control build the discipline to handle bigger challenges.

9. Continual Self-Improvement

The Stoics didn't aim for perfection—only progress (Seneca, trans. 1997). Seneca advised reflecting each evening:

- What went well today?
- What could I have done better?

Each day is another chance to improve.

Bringing It All Together: How the Four Layers Create a Stoic Life

This system makes Stoicism not just a philosophy, but a structured and applicable way of life. Instead of scattered ideas, it offers a clear, intentional approach to thinking and acting with purpose:

1. **See reality clearly** (Living in Accord with Nature—work with life, not against it).
2. **Build unshakable character** (The Four Virtues—your moral compass in every decision).
3. **Master your mindset with Stoic discipline** (The Triangle of Happiness—aligning virtue, control, and action).
4. **Reinforce resilience daily** (The Nine Core Principles—small disciplines that create lasting change).

When all four layers align, Stoicism transforms from a theory into something you embody. The question is no longer, "What does Stoicism mean?" but rather "How can I practise it today?"

The Ultimate Goal: The Path to Eudaimonia

At the heart of Stoicism lies a single goal: Eudaimonia—often translated as "flourishing" or "a life well lived." Unlike fleeting happiness, which depends on external circumstances, Eudaimonia is a deep and enduring sense of purpose, integrity, and inner tranquillity (Hadot, 1995).

The Four Layers of Stoic Practice provide a structured path to this state, turning philosophy into action. It is not something we "achieve" once, but a way of living cultivated daily through our thoughts, actions, and responses to life (Long, 2002). It is the reward for choosing reason over impulse, discipline over indulgence, and courage over avoidance (Sellars, 2006).

A Stoic does not ask, "How can I be happy?" but rather, "How can I live well?"—knowing that by focusing on virtue and right action, they naturally move toward Eudaimonia (Long, 2002).

> "You have power over your mind—not outside events. Realise this, and you will find strength."
>
> — *MARCUS AURELIUS* (AURELIUS, TRANS. 2006)

Each morning presents an opportunity to put Stoicism into practice—to strengthen character, focus on what we can control, and take deliberate action. By living this way, Eudaimonia stops being an abstract ideal and becomes an attainable state of being.

The Path Forward: Making Stoicism a Way of Life

Stoicism's true power lies not in theory but in practice. It offers a way to navigate uncertainty, build resilience, and cultivate a mindset that endures.

Whether you're encountering Stoicism for the first time or have been practicing it for years, this book provides a structured approach to integrating Stoic principles into everyday life. Rather than just exploring the philosophy, it delivers practical strategies for real-world challenges—helping you develop a mindset rooted in clarity, strength, and purpose.

In the next chapters, we'll explore how to apply these principles—turning timeless wisdom into actionable steps, ensuring Stoicism becomes more than an idea, but a way of life.

1

THE STOIC RESILIENCE TOOLKIT

FINDING STRENGTH IN ANY CHALLENGE

> "The greater the difficulty, the more glory in surmounting it. Skilful pilots gain their reputation from storms and tempests."
>
> — EPICTETUS

LIFE RARELY UNFOLDS as we expect. Careers take unexpected turns, relationships evolve, and challenges arise when we least anticipate them. Before diving into specific Stoic strategies for different life situations, it's essential to build a foundation of resilience that applies to *any* adversity.

This chapter introduces three core Stoic principles—self-care, solitude, and acceptance—as a practical toolkit for navigating uncertainty. By integrating these principles into daily life, you cultivate an inner steadiness that ensures, no matter what life brings, you remain grounded, strong, and in control.

Part One: The Self: Why Self-Care is Essential, Especially in Hardship

"Look well into yourself; there is a source of strength which will always spring up if you will always look." —Marcus Aurelius

Self-care is often dismissed as a luxury, but it is most essential when it feels least intuitive—during times of stress, uncertainty, and hardship. In difficult moments, neglecting ourselves can feel like the easier option. Discipline may feel like a burden. Yet it is precisely in these moments that we must reaffirm our inner strength and take responsibility for both mind and body (Robertson, 2019).

The Stoics did not view self-care as indulgence, but as a fundamental duty to oneself—a foundation that enables clarity, control, and resilience when life is unpredictable (Pigliucci, 2017). If we allow our minds to weaken under pressure or let our bodies deteriorate from stress, we risk becoming reactive rather than rational, fragile rather than fortified.

Three Key Pillars of Stoic Self-Care

1. **Daily reflection** – Strengthening the mind through clarity and awareness.
2. **Physical well-being** – Caring for the body to sustain resilience.
3. **Emotional balance** – Managing reactions, thoughts, and perspective.

Strengthening the Mind: The Power of Daily Reflection

> "Man conquers the world by conquering himself."
>
> — ZENO OF CITIUM

In times of uncertainty, the narrative we create in our own minds determines whether we endure with strength or collapse under pressure. The Stoics believed that daily reflection was essential for cultivating a mind that is steady, rational, and prepared for adversity (Irvine, 2008).

The Stoic Practice of Evening Reflection

Seneca made a habit of reviewing his day every evening, asking himself:

- What did I do well today?
- Where did I fall short?
- What can I improve tomorrow?

This practice is not about dwelling on mistakes or engaging in self-criticism. It is about observing ourselves honestly and making small, deliberate adjustments before emotions take over (Hadot, 1995).

How to apply this:

Set aside five minutes before bed to journal or reflect on your day. Note your thoughts, reactions, and behaviours—especially when faced with stress or setbacks. The aim is not perfection but self-awareness.

Strengthening the Body: Why Physical Well-being Matters Most in Tough Times

> "We should take wandering outdoor walks so that the mind might be nourished and refreshed by the open air and deep breathing."
>
> — SENECA

When overwhelmed, it is easy to abandon the very routines that keep us strong. Sleep, nutrition, movement—these things feel secondary when life becomes chaotic. But neglecting them only diminishes our ability to think clearly, act decisively, and remain composed (Holiday & Hanselman, 2020).

The Stoics understood that a strong body supports a strong mind. Simple, disciplined habits form the foundation of physical resilience, which in turn strengthens mental clarity (Robertson, 2019).

- **Movement** – Walking, stretching, or exercising removes mental fog and prevents stress from taking hold.
- **Controlled breathing** – Deep, measured breaths regulate emotions, lower cortisol, and restore focus (Dispenza, 2017).
- **Moderation in eating and drinking** – The Stoics valued self-control, knowing that excess weakens discipline and dulls the mind (Irvine, 2008).

In hardship, be kind to yourself and even more intentional with your energy. Taking care of yourself is not a luxury—it is an act of preparation for whatever comes next.

The Mind-Body Connection: What Science and Stoicism Agree On

> "If you are distressed by anything external, the pain is not due to the thing itself but to your estimate of it; and this you have the power to revoke at any moment."
>
> — MARCUS AURELIUS

Modern neuroscience is confirming what the Stoics understood intuitively centuries ago—our thoughts shape not just our perception but our physical health.

Dr. Joe Dispenza's research into neuroplasticity and heart-brain coherence reinforces the Stoic principle that mental discipline is essential for well-being (Dispenza, 2017).

His work demonstrates that:

- Stressful thoughts activate the body's fight-or-flight response, flooding the system with stress hormones like cortisol and adrenaline.

- Chronic stress weakens the immune system, accelerates aging, and clouds rational thinking.
- When the mind is calm and focused, the body follows, leading to lower stress levels, improved cognitive function, and increased emotional resilience.

This aligns directly with Stoic teachings—training the mind is essential, not just for emotional stability, but for physical strength and clarity.

Conversely, when the mind is calm and focused, the body follows. Dispenza's studies on heart-brain coherence show that meditative states, gratitude, and controlled breathing lead to lower stress levels, improved cognitive function, and increased emotional resilience (Dispenza, 2017).

This aligns directly with Stoic teachings—training the mind is essential not just for emotional stability, but for physical strength and clarity.

Practical Stoic Applications for Heart-Brain Coherence

1. **Controlled Breathing** – The Stoics practiced deliberate breath control, much like Dispenza's research suggests, to regulate emotions and bring the body into balance. Taking slow, deep breaths in moments of stress helps override reactive impulses (Dispenza, 2017).
2. **Mental Reframing** – By choosing how to interpret external events, we influence the body's physiological response. Viewing stressors as opportunities for growth rather than threats can significantly reduce the body's stress response (Robertson, 2019).
3. **Daily Gratitude Reflection** – Gratitude, a core practice in both Stoicism and Dispenza's work, shifts focus from what is lacking to what is present, helping to regulate emotional states and improve overall well-being (Irvine, 2008).

The Stoics remind us that suffering arises not from events themselves but from the meaning we assign to them.

By mastering our thoughts, we influence not only our mental state but also our physical resilience. Stoicism and neuroscience both agree—the mind and body are not separate. How we think determines how we feel, and ultimately, how we live.

Emotional Balance: The Power of Perspective in Hardship

> "Do not be unhappy until the bad arrives."
>
> — EPICTETUS

Difficult moments often bring emotional turbulence—fear, frustration, or the temptation to resist reality. But the Stoics teach that resilience comes from accepting what we cannot change and focusing on what is within our control (Pigliucci, 2017).

When life feels overwhelming, ask yourself:

- Is this within my control? If not, release it.
- Am I reacting emotionally or responding rationally?
- Will this matter in a week, a month, or a year?

By filtering our thoughts in this way, we prevent worry, comparison, and frustration from taking over. This is not about suppressing emotions but about choosing where to place our attention (Robertson, 2019).

The more unpredictable life becomes, the more you must anchor yourself in what you can control—your thoughts, your actions, and your well-being.

Pain is Inevitable, Suffering is Not

Pain is a natural part of life—whether physical, emotional, or circumstantial. A broken bone will ache, a betrayal will sting, and failure will disappoint. But suffering arises not from pain itself, but from our resistance to it. The mind clings to what was, to what could have been, to what it believes should be—and in doing so, magnifies distress. The Stoics understood that while we cannot always escape pain, we can free ourselves from unnecessary suffering by choosing acceptance over resistance, clarity over despair, and action over complaint (Holiday & Hanselman, 2020).

To endure pain without suffering is not to suppress emotions, but to see them for what they are—temporary visitors, not permanent residents of the mind (Hadot, 1995).

Part Two: Solitude: The Power of Stillness and Reflection

> "Nowhere can man find a quieter or more untroubled retreat than in his own soul."
>
> — MARCUS AURELIUS

Solitude is not loneliness—it is a tool for self-mastery. The Stoics saw moments of quiet as essential for self-awareness, clarity, and freedom from external validation. Yet, in the midst of turmoil, stress, or a busy day, solitude can feel like an indulgence—something we simply do not have time for. In reality, these are the moments when we need it the most.

Despite being constantly connected, many people today feel strangely isolated. This paradox highlights why deliberately choosing solitude—a focused and intentional break from external noise, expectations, and comparison—is vital for clarity, purpose, and balance (Kumar et al., 2015).

The Difference Between Solitude and Loneliness

Solitude is an intentional and enriching state, while loneliness is an unintentional and often painful response to disconnection. In a hyperconnected world, many experience surface-level interactions while feeling profoundly isolated. Japan's phenomenon of *kodokushi* (lonely death) starkly illustrates the consequences of unfulfilled social needs, revealing how digital overload can erode real-world connections (PsychCentral, 2023).

Solitude should not be seen as withdrawing from life, but as a way to reconnect with yourself. Seneca captured this idea when he advised, "Withdraw into yourself, as far as you can."

By deliberately choosing solitude, we step back from external noise and regain control over our emotions. In a world driven by constant input and comparison, it is easy to lose sight of our own values, thoughts, and direction. Solitude offers the opportunity to step back, think independently, and break free from external expectations (Hadot, 1995).

However, in times of crisis or busyness, solitude may seem unproductive—an escape, rather than a necessity. But instead of feeling guilty about taking time alone, recognise that it is a reset for the mind, allowing for better decisions and a calmer perspective (Robertson, 2019).

- Replace distractions with stillness and self-reflection to break free from the constant need for approval.
- Use solitude to observe thoughts rather than be consumed by them.

> "He who follows reason in all things is both tranquil and active at the same time."
>
> — MARCUS AURELIUS

Building Inner Strength Through Solitude

The Stoics understood that moments of solitude strengthen the mind and prepare us for life's challenges.

Solitude is not about permanent withdrawal, but about intentional moments of quiet to process experiences, gain perspective, and reinforce inner peace against external chaos.

Practical ways to cultivate solitude:

- Dedicate short periods of intentional solitude each day, free from distractions.
- Use quiet moments to reaffirm your values and cultivate resilience.
- Reflect on your reactions, thoughts, and decisions without external influence.

Balancing Solitude and Technology

Technology has paradoxically both diminished and enhanced our ability to be alone. While social media and constant notifications intrude on solitude, digital tools can also be used intentionally to support mindfulness and self-reflection.

The key is balance:

- Use technology as a tool, not a crutch.
- Set boundaries on when and how you engage with digital distractions.
- Schedule deliberate disconnection, even if only for a few minutes at a time.

Why Your Brain Craves Silence

Neuroscience has revealed that solitude is deeply restorative. When the brain is free from external stimulation, it activates the default mode network (DMN)—the system responsible for:

- Self-reflection
- Memory consolidation
- Creative problem-solving

Studies show that moments of quiet reduce stress, enhance mental clarity, and improve decision-making (Kumar et al., 2015; PsychCentral, 2023). Despite these benefits, modern society often judges stillness as unproductive, reinforcing the false idea that busyness equals worth.

The Busyness Trap and the Power of Stillness

Many cultures equate constant activity with self-worth, making solitude seem like idleness. However, some of the most successful and visionary individuals have embraced solitude as a strategic tool:

- Bill Gates dedicates "think weeks" to deep reflection.
- Maya Angelou created isolated workspaces to enhance creativity.
- Einstein credited moments of solitude with some of his greatest insights.

Even in busy lives, small intentional moments of solitude—a few deep breaths, a pause before starting the day, or a break from noise—can have profound effects.

Returning to Yourself Through Stillness

Tomorrow, set aside just ten minutes of absolute solitude. No phone, no distractions—just you. Sit with your thoughts. Observe what emerges.

At first, it may feel unfamiliar—even uncomfortable. But in time, you will realise that silence is not empty—it is full of possibility.

Solitude is not a retreat from the world—it is a return to yourself. When used wisely, solitude strengthens not only resilience but also clarity, creativity, and emotional independence. These moments of stillness allow us to process experiences, recalibrate our minds, and reconnect with what truly matters. Max Ehrmann captures it beautifully. "Go placidly amid the noise and haste, and remember what peace there may be in silence."

Part Three: The Unexpected: Accepting When Life Doesn't Go to Plan

> "The impediment to action advances action. What stands in the way becomes the way."
>
> — MARCUS AURELIUS

Life is unpredictable. When things go wrong, we often resist, compare ourselves to others, or become consumed by frustration. The Stoic response is to accept, adapt, and use adversity as an opportunity for growth. (Irvine, 2008)

This section explores how to apply Stoic resilience when facing setbacks, ensuring that challenges become opportunities for strength rather than sources of despair.

Four Stoic Principles for Navigating Setbacks

1. ***Amor Fati*** – Accept the situation for what it is. Resist the urge to fight reality or dwell on "what should have been." Once you embrace the situation, you can begin to move forward.
2. **Focus on Your Own Judgement** – Free yourself from concern over what others think of your circumstances.
3. **Avoid Comparison** – Looking at others' lives only distorts your perspective and adds unnecessary suffering.
4. **Be Mindful About Sharing** – Sharing too much can bring unwanted judgment or advice that does not serve you.

Finding Strength in Chaos: Embracing *Amor Fati*

The essence of *Amor Fati* lies in accepting fate and navigating life's chaos with resilience and grace. It shifts focus to our thoughts, actions, and responses, rather than external circumstances that lie beyond our control.

For example:

- **Marcus Aurelius** governed during plagues and wars, yet his *Meditations* reflect a profound calm, rooted in acceptance of the turbulence of his time.
- **Malala Yousafzai** survived a near-fatal attack and turned her trauma into a global movement for girls' education (Yousafzai & Lamb, 2013).

Both figures exemplify how deeply held values—whether Stoic philosophy or a belief in universal education—provide the strength to transform adversity into impactful action.

Practical Guidance for Practising *Amor Fati*

- **Focus on the Present Moment** – Chaos often overwhelms us when we fixate on the past or future. Ground yourself in what can be done now.
- **Anchor Yourself in Your Values** – When everything feels unstable, your values remain a compass.
- **Practice Detachment** – Recognise what is within your control, and let go of what is not.
- **Find Meaning in Adversity** – Ask yourself, *What lesson can I learn from this?*
- **Seek Inner Peace Through Routine** – In uncertain times, small daily practices—such as journaling or exercise—provide stability.

By applying *Amor Fati*, difficulties become a part of your story, not the entirety of it.

Consider the story of Thomas Edison. After countless failed attempts to create a working light bulb, he famously reframed his failures, saying, "I have not failed. I've just found 10,000 ways that won't work."

His persistence and ability to view setbacks as part of the process ultimately led to one of the most transformative inventions in history.

Liberating Yourself from Comparison and the Judgement of Others

One of the most painful aspects of life not going according to plan is the fear of judgement from others. Whether it is a job loss, delayed milestones, or personal failures, we often torment ourselves with imagined judgments.

> "You are in the habit of comparing yourself with others, and this causes you pain. You will always find someone who is richer, smarter, or better looking. Stop focusing on others and focus on your own progress instead."
>
> — SENECA

However, Stoicism offers wisdom to free us from this burden.

> "If you are ever tempted to look for outside approval, realise that you have compromised your integrity."
>
> — EPICTETUS

Practical Guidance to Detach from Imagined Judgments

- **Ask yourself:** Is this thought based on fact, or am I projecting my own insecurities?
- **Reaffirm Your Values** – If your actions align with your principles, the opinions of others lose their significance.
- **Practice Indifference** – The Stoic concept of *apatheia* (freedom from passion) teaches us to let go of unnecessary concerns about what others think.

- **Remember: Most People Are Focused on Themselves** – My mum once said, "People are just too busy to notice your life. Ask them a question about theirs, and they will talk for hours."

Similarly, comparison is one of the greatest sources of dissatisfaction in life. When things go wrong, seeing others succeed where we struggle deepens frustration.

"Look inward; do not compare yourself to others. Each day provides its own gifts." — Marcus Aurelius

Why Comparison is Especially Harmful During Tough Times

1. **It Magnifies Feelings of Failure** – Seeing someone else thrive when we are struggling can amplify self-doubt.
2. **It Overlooks Personal Context** – Everyone's life is shaped by unique circumstances.
3. **It Distracts from Recovery** – Comparing ourselves to others shifts focus away from taking action.
4. **It Creates a False Narrative** – Social media presents an illusion, making others' lives look effortless.

Practical Steps to Overcome Comparison

- **Celebrate Your Own Milestones** – Even small progress counts.
- **Limit Social Media Exposure** – Recognise the distortion and set boundaries.
- **Reframe Envy as Inspiration** – Instead of feeling threatened by others' success, ask: *What can I learn from them?*
- **Focus on Your Values** – When your life aligns with your values, external comparisons lose their power.
- **Practice Gratitude** – Each day, acknowledge what you have achieved, even if small.

When life is going well, comparison might seem harmless, even motivating. But when things go wrong, it can erode self-esteem and hope. Instead, turn inward—focus on what you can control and measure success by how true you are to yourself.

The Power of Silence: Don't Overshare During Tough Times

Restraint in speech is a Stoic discipline. When life does not go as planned, oversharing struggles can deplete energy and invite unnecessary judgment. Resisting the urge to overshare is a powerful act of self-discipline. When life doesn't go as planned, venting can feel like relief—but too often, it distracts us from actual problem-solving and drains mental energy.

While seeking support is valuable, excessive sharing—especially online—can invite unwanted opinions, unhelpful advice, or even reinforce negative emotions. Stoicism teaches that true resilience is built internally, not in validation from others (Irvine, 2008).

Practical Steps to Practise Restraint

- **Pause Before Speaking or Posting** – Ask, *Will this help me resolve the issue or just reinforce my frustration?*
- **Choose Your Audience Wisely** – Seek trusted confidants, not just anyone who will listen.
- **Focus on Solutions** – Shift conversations from complaints to action.

Conclusion: The Inner Citadel – Strength That Endures

The Stoics spoke of the Inner Citadel—a fortress within the mind, immune to the chaos of the external world. It is the part of us that cannot be broken by fortune, failure, or fear. Seneca described it as a place of refuge, where the wise retreat not to escape life, but to meet it with greater strength (Hadot, 1995). Marcus Aurelius reinforced this idea, reminding himself that true peace is not found in distant retreats or quiet landscapes, but within his own reasoned mind (Robertson, 2019).

Pain will visit us all—this is beyond our control. *Pain is inevitable. But suffering? That is a choice.* Events themselves are neutral; it is our judgment of them that determines whether they crush us or make us stronger. The moment we detach from our impulses and accept reality as it is, we begin to build the Inner Citadel—brick by brick, through every hardship we endure with wisdom and clarity.

This fortress is not built in comfort. It is formed in every moment we choose self-discipline over indulgence, perspective over panic, action over complaint.

It is the unshakable core we cultivate within ourselves—a mind fortified by reason, a soul anchored in resilience (Pigliucci, 2017).

> "The nearer a man comes to a calm mind, the closer he is to strength."
>
> — MARCUS AURELIUS

Master the mind, master the moment—and you will remain unshaken, no matter what unfolds.

2

THE STOIC'S GUIDE TO THRIVING IN THE MODERN WORKPLACE

> "Whatever anyone does or says, I must be emerald and keep my colour."
>
> — MARCUS AURELIUS

THE TRADITIONAL WORKPLACE is undergoing a profound and unprecedented transformation.

First, the COVID-19 pandemic forced millions of us into remote work, stripping away traditional structures of support and accountability. Just as we adapted, another seismic shift arrived: AI—promising efficiency but threatening job security, forcing workers to redefine their roles amidst uncertainty.

Work-life balance, while idealized, remains elusive—overshadowed by a busyness culture that equates overloaded schedules with self-worth (Newport, 2016). We are urged to work smarter, not harder, yet we are judged if we don't appear busy or if we prioritize family over late-night availability (Pang, 2019).

As traditional working structures crumble, anxiety grows: *Will my job survive? How do I remain relevant? Am I already obsolete?* The relentless pace of change has turned the workplace into a battleground, exposing a stark divide: those who evolve through resilience and strategic upskilling, and those who resist until they are inevitably left behind.

> "Begin each day by telling yourself: today I shall be meeting with interference, ingratitude, insolence, disloyalty, ill-will, and selfishness."
>
> — MARCUS AURELIUS

Marcus Aurelius' wisdom has never been more relevant. The modern workplace is not just a place of employment—it is a test of character. Professionals must navigate corporate politics, shifting company priorities, and economic uncertainties while maintaining composure and resilience.

This is where Stoic steadiness becomes essential. The workplace will always present external pressures—difficult colleagues, sudden policy changes, and unpredictable challenges—but true stability comes from within.

Marcus Aurelius' opening quote is a powerful reminder: just as an emerald remains unchanged by its surroundings, we too must hold firm to our values. True resilience in the workplace means maintaining composure, integrity, and authenticity—no matter the chaos around us.

Work is no longer just a means of survival—it has become a stage for personal growth, demanding more than just technical adaptability. To not just survive but thrive, it requires a Stoic mindset.

For the Stoics, work was never just about survival—it was a stage for cultivating resilience, patience, and integrity. These virtues, once central to ancient philosophy, are now more critical than ever for professional success (Robertson, 2019).

Let's look at how Stoicism can help in this environment.

Stoic Armour for the Workplace Revolution

Here is your workplace armour to thrive in the workplace:

1. **Embrace Change** - Evolution is key to survival
2. **Set Clear Boundaries** - Self-respect is the foundation of sustainable success
3. **Cultivate Strategic Trust** - Create a safe space for openness and growth.
4. **Embody Integrity** - Strengthen your credibility for long-term success.
5. **Elevate emotional discipline** - Project strength and maintain composure under pressure.

Let's explore these tenets, as active strategies for redefining success in an era of upheaval.

1. Embrace Change

In our rapidly evolving workplace, those who fear change risk stagnation and even redundancy, while those who adapt thrive. As the Stoics emphasise, change is a natural force: it only becomes an existential threat in the workplace if we don't embrace it (Irvine, 2008).

The modern workforce demands agility. AI-driven automation, economic shifts, and hybrid work models necessitate continuous upskilling (Schwab, 2017). Instead of fearing obsolescence, professionals should actively invest in learning and career adaptability (Newport, 2016).

Demonstrating adaptability will not only safeguard your career but also enhance your sense of autonomy and resilience in an uncertain world. Take the initiative by expressing your willingness to undertake training in performance reviews, volunteering for new tasks that require upskilling, and actively seeking mentorship or professional development opportunities.

By doing so, you position yourself as a proactive and indispensable asset in a constantly evolving workplace.

2. Set Clear Boundaries -Self-respect is the foundation of sustainable success

Establishing workplace boundaries protects well-being by preventing burnout, fostering respect, and maintaining a healthy work-life balance (Pang, 2019).

While Stoic philosophy does not explicitly mention boundaries, its core tenets—self-mastery, rational decision-making, and discipline—align with the need to set limits in the modern workplace (Hadot, 1995).

In a hyper-connected era, many professionals feel pressured to be constantly available, leading to chronic stress and reduced efficiency (Newport, 2016). However, establishing clear boundaries does not mean disengagement—it means sustainable success.

However, setting boundaries does not mean jeopardising your job security. If your productivity is demonstrable, your value is clear—and upskilling to enhance productivity can reinforce your position. Strong boundaries are not about resistance; they are about creating sustainable work habits that prevent burnout and improve long-term performance.

One effective technique is to avoid over-explaining. Instead of lengthy justifications, be concise yet professional while considering your workplace dynamics.

If you need to defer a task:

"I don't have the capacity right now, but I'd be happy to help once X is completed."

If prioritization needs to be clarified:

"I want to make sure I'm focusing on the highest-priority tasks. Would you like me to shift my focus from Y to this instead?"

This approach is accommodating yet assertive—balancing workplace expectations with self-preservation. Protecting your time and energy is essential for sustained productivity, resilience, and peace of mind. Of course, every workplace is different. Use these techniques in a way that aligns with your company culture and professional judgment.

3. Cultivate Strategic Trust

Building trust with the right people creates a safe space for openness and growth.

Trust is a powerful yet fragile currency in the workplace. While collaboration and strong relationships are essential for success, not everyone has your best interests at heart. Epictetus reminds us: “Be discriminating about what you entrust and to whom.” In an environment driven by competition, office politics, and shifting loyalties, discretion is not just advisable—it is necessary.

Blind trust can lead to misaligned expectations or workplace politics (Grant, 2013). This does not mean adopting a cynical view of colleagues, but rather practising measured trust—one built on consistency, reliability, and demonstrated integrity. Instead of confiding in everyone, observe how people behave under pressure. Do they honour confidences? Do they stand by their values, or do they shift allegiances when convenient?

At the same time, avoiding trust altogether is a mistake. Isolation in the workplace can lead to missed opportunities for mentorship, collaboration, and support. The key is to foster relationships with those who have earned your confidence.

A few guiding Stoic principles can help navigate trust issues with wisdom:

Observe before confiding – Pay attention to how someone treats others before trusting them with sensitive information.

Build trust gradually – based on colleagues repeated actions, not just words.

Maintain professional boundaries – Even in close workplace relationships, don't overshare—avoid situations e.g., such as excess alcohol on a work night out-where this might occur. Healthy boundaries ensure your integrity is not compromised and your position remains protected.

Act with honesty and consistency – Just as you judge others, ensure that you yourself are a trustworthy colleague.

By being discerning in who you trust and how much you share, you safeguard both your professional reputation and your peace of mind.

4. Embody Integrity

Integrity builds trust, credibility, and long-term success by ensuring ethical, principled decisions in the workplace.

"Integrity is doing the right thing, even when no one is watching."

This quote is often attributed to C.S. Lewis, though its origins remain uncertain. I would go further: integrity is the ultimate test of self-discipline (or mastery). It is tested in solitude, where there is no audience, no reward, and no consequence—only the quiet weight of our own principles. True self-mastery is not about external validation but the inner discipline to act correctly, regardless of recognition. The highest form of integrity is when it ceases to be a choice and becomes who we are.

But integrity is not tested when things are easy—it is tested in the face of injustice, betrayal, and adversity. The real measure of character is how we respond when no one is watching.

Marcus Aurelius reminds us: "The best way of avenging yourself is not to become like the wrongdoer." The greatest challenge in the modern workplace is not just to survive, but to do so without compromising your character. The rules of work are shifting—loyalty is conditional, power is fleeting, and self-interest often prevails—but your integrity must remain unshakable.

Seneca wrote, "A good character, when established, is not easily overthrown." You will encounter deceit, office politics, and those who act without honour—but your strength lies in refusing to mirror their ways.

This does not mean being passive. Stand firm. Uphold your values. Meet hostility with wisdom, not retaliation. Stoicism teaches that true power lies in self-mastery—not in controlling others, but in refusing to let them control you.

Integrity is not weakness—it is the ultimate strength.

5. Elevate Emotional Discipline: The Power of HPF (Happy Professional Face)

Mastering emotional self-discipline in the workplace builds resilience, sharpens decision-making, and ensures composure under pressure. It not only leads to professional success but also projects an image of strength and credibility.

Emotional discipline is not a single skill but a framework—a collection of interdependent principles that, when practiced together, create a powerful foundation for maintaining composure and resilience in professional settings.

A key tool for emotional mastery is Happy Professional Face (HPF)—a composed, professional demeanour that projects confidence and stability, even in high-pressure situations.

What is HPF?

HPF is a workplace resilience strategy that I developed to help professionals maintain composure, confidence, and credibility under pressure. It is not about forced positivity or emotional suppression—it is about self-regulation and strategic composure.

Key Elements of HPF:

- **Handling Criticism Effectively** – Responding with logic, not emotion.
- **Preparing for Setbacks** – Anticipating challenges before they arise.
- **Focusing on What You Can Control** – Choosing rational responses over emotional reactions.

By practicing HPF, professionals:

- Project resilience and composure.
- Command respect through professionalism.
- Strengthen credibility and career longevity.

> "The nearer a man comes to a calm mind, the closer he is to strength."
>
> — MARCUS AURELIUS

By mastering HPF, we do not ignore difficulties—we face them with clarity, confidence, and control.

1. Handling Criticism Effectively

Criticism is inevitable in a high-pressure work environment, but how you respond defines your professional strength. Emotions can cloud judgment, leading to impulsive reactions. Instead of reacting with frustration or defensiveness, cultivate emotional discipline—respond with logic, not impulse.

- **Distinguish Between Constructive and Destructive Criticism.** Not all criticism is valid. To differentiate, ask yourself: Does this feedback provide specific, actionable points for improvement? Is it given with the intent to help you grow? Constructive criticism aims to refine skills and enhance performance, whereas baseless criticism is often vague, personal, or intended to undermine (Grant, 2013). If feedback is constructive, embrace it as a tool for development. If it lacks substance or is rooted in negativity, discard it and refocus on your goals. Do not let unfounded opinions dictate your self-worth.

- **Recognise the Insecurities of Others.** Workplace insecurities can drive people to undermine others. Recognise that their negativity is often a reflection of their own fears rather than a judgment of your abilities. To determine if their words stem from insecurity, observe patterns in their behaviour. Are they frequently critical of others? Do they avoid constructive discussion or react defensively when questioned? Does their criticism lack substance or focus on personal rather than professional aspects? These signs suggest their negativity is more about them than about you. By applying Stoic detachment, which is further explored below, you can acknowledge their words without allowing them to affect your self-respect (Hadot, 1995).

2. Preparing for Setbacks and Adversity

The Stoic practice of *premeditatio malorum*—the premeditation of adversity—teaches us to anticipate difficulties before they arise. This mindset helps you remain composed and steady rather than reacting with fear or frustration when challenges emerge (Irvine, 2008).

Anticipating challenges requires a proactive mindset—one that prepares for potential difficulties without succumbing to paranoia or negativity. As Marcus Aurelius advises, recognising workplace struggles while maintaining composure enables rational and strategic responses instead of emotional reactions (Robertson, 2019).

Transitioning from an emotional reaction to a strategic

response involves taking a deliberate pause, assessing the situation objectively, and considering the broader implications before acting. This process includes scenario planning, assessing risks, mentally rehearsing solutions, and focusing on what can be controlled rather than reacting impulsively.

To anticipate and stay ahead of potential setbacks, it helps to proactively seek insights from industry trends, professional networks, and internal company communications. Engaging in think tanks, discussion groups, and cross-functional projects fosters awareness of upcoming shifts, enabling strategic adaptation. Instead of dwelling on perceived threats or workplace injustices, channel energy into constructive responses: seek mentorship for guidance, develop contingency plans, and build skills that enhance adaptability.

3. Focussing on Controlling What You Can, Letting Go of What You Can't

Epictetus reminds us:

> "The chief task in life is simply this: to identify and separate matters so that I can say clearly to myself which are externals not under my control, and which have to do with the choices I actually control."
>
> — EPICTETUS (TRANS. 1995)

Recognise What Is Beyond Your Control

Office politics, corporate restructuring, and market fluctuations are external forces that you cannot change. Wasting energy on these uncertainties only leads to frustration (Hadot, 1995).

Work Out What You Can Control

A simple way to determine what is within your control is to ask yourself:

- Do I have direct influence over this? If yes, focus on taking decisive action.
- Can I indirectly influence the outcome? If so, consider efforts you can make while accepting that success isn't guaranteed.
- Would my actions realistically change the result? If no, let go of unnecessary worry and focus on areas where your efforts have impact.
- Am I focusing on the problem or my response to it? If you're fixated on external factors, shift your attention to managing your reaction effectively (Irvine, 2008).

Practically, listing workplace challenges into three categories—things you control, things you influence, and things outside your control—helps in allocating your energy wisely. This ensures that you concentrate efforts on meaningful actions rather than dwelling on external uncertainties.

A Final Word: The Power of Mindful Detachment

Be brave. These are hostile times—put on your Stoic armour and fight the good fight. Not through conflict, but through discipline, wisdom, and resilience.

At the heart of this is Mindful Detachment—not just a skill, but a guiding philosophy. It is the discipline of stepping back, assessing situations with clarity, and focusing energy where it truly matters (Pigliucci, 2017). It is not disengagement, but control—choosing response over reaction, and clarity over chaos.

Throughout this chapter, we've explored detachment as a practical tool—how to embrace change, set clear boundaries, cultivate strategic trust, embody integrity, and elevate emotional discipline, focusing on what you can control. But true mastery comes when detachment is no longer just a conscious effort but an instinctive mindset (Robertson, 2019). The workplace will continue to evolve in unpredictable ways, but your ability to remain composed and adaptive is within your command.

By internalising Mindful Detachment, you cultivate resilience, protect your mental energy, and refuse to be pulled into unnecessary turmoil. It allows you to respond with intention rather than impulse, to choose clarity over reactivity, and to act with purpose instead of being driven by external pressures.

Let composure be your strength, integrity your guide, and adaptability your greatest asset.

3

NAVIGATING FRIENDSHIPS

WISDOM FOR MEANINGFUL CONNECTIONS

"The key is to keep company only with people who uplift you, whose presence calls forth your best."

— EPICTETUS (TRANS. 2008)

The Key to Meaningful Friendships

FRIENDSHIP IS one of the most enriching aspects of life, offering connection, support, and mutual growth. The relationships we choose to nurture can uplift and inspire us, shaping our journey in profound ways. However, just as healthy friendships contribute to our well-being, some connections may no longer align with our values or personal growth.

We invest time and energy into our friendships, hoping they will provide joy and encouragement. While some relationships flourish, others may become unbalanced or draining. Recognizing which friendships to cultivate and which to release is an essential part of fostering a meaningful social circle that enhances our lives.

In this chapter, we will explore how to identify and nurture meaningful friendships, navigate challenges, and develop the courage to let go of relationships that no longer serve our well-being. By approaching friendship with intentionality, we create space for deeper connections that bring joy, resilience, and fulfilment.

The Art of Friendship

Friendship is one of life's most cherished gifts, yet it is often taken for granted. While some friendships endure through life's storms, others falter when tested. The Stoics, though often seen as solitary philosophers, had profound insights into building and sustaining meaningful relationships. Their wisdom remains as relevant today as ever.

Seneca advises us to be discerning when choosing our friends. Before offering someone our trust, we should judge their character: Are they honest? Do they act with integrity? Will they stand by us in difficult times? As he notes, "Associate with those who will make a better person of you. Welcome those whom you yourself can improve. The process is mutual; for men learn while they teach" (Seneca, trans. 1917). A true friend is steadfast and loyal, offering more than fleeting companionship.

However, some relationships falter under scrutiny. The so-called fair-weather friend—someone who is present during good times but absent in hardship—is not uncommon. True friendship is not transactional; it is about mutual support and shared commitment, not what one person can gain from the other.

Sometimes, the hardest choice is to let go of friendships that no longer serve us. As Epictetus teaches, we must prioritize our growth and peace over misplaced loyalty to relationships that drain us. Marcus Aurelius similarly advises, "If your cucumber is bitter, throw it away. If there are brambles in your path, go around them. That is enough. Do not ask, 'Why do such things exist?'" (Aurelius, trans. 2002). Life's brevity underscores the importance of surrounding ourselves with those who bring joy, understanding, and encouragement.

The Importance of Nurturing Childhood Friendships

As Seneca wisely counselled, "One of the most beautiful qualities of true friendship is to understand and be understood" (Seneca, trans. 1917). This is particularly true of childhood friends, who hold a unique and irreplaceable role in our lives. They often know us better than anyone, having witnessed the unfiltered version of ourselves before the layers of adulthood—careers, personas, and responsibilities—took shape. They understand the nuances of our family dynamics, our early triumphs and struggles, and the foundational values that shaped who we are.

In challenging times, childhood friends can provide invaluable insights into our behaviours, reminding us of our core identity and offering perspectives that others cannot. These bonds, forged in formative years, are a treasure worth cherishing. As life progresses, making time to nurture these relationships ensures that we maintain connections to our true selves and to the people who knew us at our most authentic.

Building a Supportive Network

A supportive network is essential for a fulfilling and resilient life. True friendship, according to the Stoics, is not about quantity but about virtue. It is not merely about having people around but about fostering relationships rooted in mutual respect, wisdom, and encouragement (Seneca, trans. 1917).

In modern terms, virtue refers to the qualities that make someone a trustworthy, ethical, and positive presence in your life—integrity, honesty, kindness, wisdom, and resilience. These are the traits that define a true friend and contribute to a healthy, enriching relationship.

Start by identifying individuals who align with your values and bring tranquillity and growth into your life. Nurture these relationships by practicing active listening, showing empathy, and being present. Seek to surround yourself with people who challenge you to improve, celebrate your successes without envy, and stand by you in adversity.

As Marcus Aurelius reminds us: "The soul becomes dyed with the colour of its thoughts" (Aurelius, trans. 2002). The people you spend time with shape your mindset and well-being. Therefore, be discerning about who you allow into your inner circle and focus on virtue over status or convenience. Building a supportive network is an ongoing process, but its rewards are enduring—a community that uplifts you and provides strength through life's challenges.

Quality Over Quantity

In an age dominated by social media, the number of "friends" or followers we have is often seen as a measure of success. But Stoicism teaches that true friendship is based on depth, not breadth. As Seneca states, "It is not the number of friends, but the virtue of friends, that counts." – Seneca (trans. 1917)

A handful of loyal, genuine friends is far more valuable than a large social circle filled with superficial connections. True friendships are built on mutual respect, honesty, and shared principles. A true friend is a steady anchor, offering unwavering support during life's storms. Instead of striving for quantity, focus on nurturing a small circle of friends who genuinely align with your values.

Identifying Toxic Relationships

Not all friendships are healthy, and Stoicism teaches us to cultivate relationships that contribute to our inner peace. A toxic friendship disrupts tranquillity and prevents us from focusing on what truly matters. Here are some signs of an unhealthy friendship:

1. **Emotional Drainage**: Do you feel exhausted or anxious after spending time with this person? True

friends leave you feeling supported and uplifted, not depleted.

2. **Lack of Reciprocity:** A healthy friendship involves a balance of give and take. If you're always the one giving, whether it's time, energy, or emotional support, it may be time to re-evaluate.
3. **Negativity and Drama** – Stoicism teaches us to avoid needless suffering. If a friend consistently brings chaos, pessimism, or conflict, they are harming your peace of mind.
4. **Boundary Violations:** A true friend respects your boundaries, whether they pertain to your time, emotions, or personal space. Repeated disregard for boundaries is a red flag.
5. **Broken Trust:** Trust is the foundation of any relationship. If a friend regularly betrays your confidence or undermines you, the relationship may no longer be worth maintaining.

Even when we recognize an unhealthy friendship, letting go can feel overwhelming. We often hold onto toxic relationships for several reasons:

- **Fear of Loneliness** – The idea of being alone can be daunting, but staying in a toxic friendship can lead to even greater feelings of isolation.
- **Cognitive Dissonance** – We rationalize harmful behaviour to avoid facing the truth. For example, we might tell ourselves, *"They're just joking"* or *"They're going through a tough time."*
- **Fear of Confrontation** – Many people avoid addressing toxic dynamics because they fear conflict or drama.
- **Hope for Change** – We may cling to the belief that the friend will eventually change or improve. While growth is possible, it's often unrealistic to wait for someone else to change.

As Seneca reminds us, "You must forgive many things in others, but nothing in yourself" (Seneca, trans. 1917).

While compassion for others is important, we must not excuse ongoing harm at the expense of our own well-being. Recognizing these psychological barriers is the first step toward freeing ourselves from unhealthy relationships.

How to Leave a Toxic Friendship: A Stoic Approach

1. Assess the Energy Exchange:

Reflect on how the friendship makes you feel. Does it align with virtue and peace of mind?

> "Consider, when you judge whether to admit someone to your friendship, that you are making a commitment to your own peace of mind."
>
> — SENECA

2. Acknowledge the Need for Change:

Recognize that outgrowing friendships is natural.
Let go without anger:

> "Do not hate them, but detach from them with indifference."
>
> — EPICTETUS

3. Create Emotional and Physical Distance:

Start by gradually reducing the amount of time you spend with the person. Politely decline plans or limit the duration of your interactions.

Avoid engaging deeply in conversations that drain you or lead to unnecessary conflict.

4. Communicate with Clarity (If Necessary):

If the friendship has redeemable qualities, have an honest conversation

Use calm, non-judgmental language to share your feelings. For example: *"I've been feeling overwhelmed lately, and I think I need to take some space to focus on myself. I value the time we've shared, but I need to prioritise my well-being right now."*

Avoid accusations or blaming language, as this can escalate the situation.

5. Set and Enforce Boundaries:

Be clear about behaviours you will not tolerate.

Toxic individuals often push back when you assert boundaries —stand firm.

6. Let the Friendship Fade (If Confrontation Is Unnecessary):

If a direct conversation is not needed, allow the relationship to drift naturally.

If the friendship is irreparably toxic and you don't feel safe or comfortable confronting them, let the relationship naturally drift apart. Reduce contact by no longer initiating conversations, responding less frequently, or declining invitations.

7. Seek Support and Reflect:

Seek support from other friends (while respecting boundaries), mentors, or a therapist for guidance.

Reflect on what you learned about boundaries and self-respect.

8. Focus on Positivity and Growth:

Redirect the time and energy you've freed up toward

relationships and activities that enrich your life. Strengthen connections with supportive friends, pursue hobbies, or work on personal development.

Celebrate small wins as you regain your emotional balance and peace.

9. Accept the Emotional Impact:

Allow yourself to grieve the end of the friendship, even if it was unhealthy. It's normal to feel a mix of sadness, relief, and guilt.

Remind yourself that leaving was an act of self-respect, not cruelty, and that you deserve friendships rooted in mutual care and support.

10. Move Forward with Clarity:

As Marcus Aurelius advises, "Receive without pride, let go without attachment" (Aurelius, trans. 2002).

Embrace the freedom that comes with releasing what no longer serves you.

Redirect the time and energy you've freed up toward relationships and activities that enrich your life. Strengthen connections with supportive friends, pursue hobbies, or work on personal development.

Celebrate small wins as you regain your emotional balance and peace.

The Pain of Betrayal in Friendship

Discovering that a friend has betrayed you is a deeply painful experience. Betrayal shatters the foundation of trust that friendships are built on, leaving behind feelings of hurt, confusion, and sometimes anger. This emotional upheaval can feel similar to, if not more intense than, other types of relationship betrayals because of the vulnerability and shared history involved.

The Stoics offer guidance for navigating the pain of betrayal.

While they do not diminish the hurt, they emphasize the importance of maintaining perspective and regaining control over our emotions (Aurelius, trans. 2002).

Here are some Stoic-inspired strategies to help you process and move forward:

1. Acknowledge the Pain Without Dwelling on It:

Betrayal hurts, and it's important to validate those feelings rather than suppress them. Marcus Aurelius reminds us, "You have power over your mind—not outside events. Realize this, and you will find strength." Acknowledge the hurt, but don't let it consume you.

2. Reflect on the Reality of Human Imperfection:

The Stoics believed in accepting human fallibility. People, even those we trust, can make mistakes or acting out of self-interest. Seneca advises, "You must live for others if you wish to live for yourself" (Seneca, trans. 1917). This doesn't mean condoning betrayal but recognizing that others' actions often stem from their own weaknesses, fears, or desires, not a reflection of your worth.

3. Focus on What You Can Control:

While you can't change the betrayal or the friend's behaviour, you can control your response. Epictetus advises, "It's not what happens to you, but how you react to it that matters" (Epictetus, trans. 2008). Channel your energy into actions that protect your peace and foster your growth.

4. Reassess and Rebuild Your Boundaries:

Betrayal is an opportunity to evaluate the boundaries you have set in your relationships. Were there red flags you ignored? Did you allow this person too much access to your trust and vulnerability without reciprocation? Use this experience to strengthen boundaries, ensuring that future friendships are based on mutual respect, integrity, and alignment with your values (Seneca, trans. 1917)

5. **Seek Growth Through Adversity:**

Painful experiences can be profound teachers. Instead of viewing betrayal as a purely negative event, Stoicism encourages us to extract wisdom from suffering. As Seneca wrote:

"Difficulties strengthen the mind, as labour does the body" (Seneca, trans. 1917).

Reflect on what this betrayal has taught you about trust, resilience, and your own capacity to heal.

6. **Act with Dignity:**

When betrayed, it can be tempting to react emotionally—whether through anger, retaliation, or social media rants. However, Stoicism teaches restraint. Marcus Aurelius advises: "The best revenge is to be unlike him who performed the injury" (Aurelius, trans. 2002).

By rising above pettiness, you preserve your integrity and demonstrate strength. True resilience is not in seeking retribution, but in proving that betrayal does not diminish your character.

Final Reflection

Betrayal is a wound that takes time to heal, but with reflection and resilience, it can also become a catalyst for personal growth. Remember, you are not defined by someone else's actions, and you have the strength to move forward with clarity and dignity.

When Loyalties Are Tested: Setting Boundaries with Integrity

There may be moments in friendships when your loyalties are tested—when a friend's actions, such as having an affair or lying about other important issues, put you in a compromising position. These situations can be deeply uncomfortable, particularly if they threaten to erode trust within a larger social circle or conflict with your personal values. Handling these moments with care, integrity, and wisdom is crucial.

1. Clarify Your Own Values

Begin by reflecting on your principles and how the situation aligns or conflicts with them. The Stoics emphasize living in accordance with virtue. As Marcus Aurelius states:

"If it is not right, do not do it; if it is not true, do not say it" (Aurelius, trans. 2002).

Allow your values to guide your actions. If a friend's behaviour contradicts your moral compass, recognize that you are not obligated to compromise your integrity for the sake of loyalty.

2. Set Firm Boundaries

If your friend's actions are pulling you into their deception or compromising your integrity, establish clear boundaries. This may involve letting them know you cannot be complicit in their behaviour without passing judgment. As Epictetus advises: "Know first who you are and then adorn yourself accordingly" (Epictetus, trans. 2008).

Staying true to your identity and moral compass will help you navigate these situations with confidence.

3. Communicate with Compassion

Approach your friend with honesty and empathy. Explain how their behaviour affects you and why you must take a step back or refrain from involvement. Avoid accusations or emotional escalation, focusing instead on maintaining respect. Thoughtful communication allows you to express your position without creating unnecessary conflict.

4. Understand Their Limitations

A friend's poor choices often reflect their struggles or personal limitations. While this does not excuse harmful behaviour, recognizing this can help you avoid personalizing their actions. As Marcus Aurelius reminds us: "Whenever someone has done wrong by you, immediately consider what notion of good or evil they had in doing it" (Aurelius, trans. 2002, p. 94).

Their behaviour is shaped by their own beliefs, experiences, and struggles—not necessarily by a desire to harm you. Understanding their flaws does not mean you must tolerate them indefinitely. Instead, view their actions as a reflection of their own challenges, rather than a personal betrayal.

5. Decide When to Step Away

If a friend's actions persist and continue to compromise your peace or values, it may be necessary to distance yourself. This does not have to be dramatic; instead, let it be a quiet affirmation of your commitment to integrity. Marcus Aurelius offers wisdom here: "Waste no more time arguing about what a good man should be. Be one" (Aurelius, trans. 2002).

By focusing on your own character, you lead by example. Sometimes, the most effective way to demonstrate virtue is to uphold it unwaveringly, even if it means walking away from relationships that do not align with it.

When loyalties are tested, remember that prioritizing your values does not mean abandoning compassion. Instead, it involves balancing empathy with self-respect, ensuring your actions align with your principles while treating others with dignity.

When Friends Lose Touch: Navigating the Distance

Friendships, even the strongest ones, can sometimes falter due to life's changing circumstances. When an important friend drifts away, it can feel painful and confusing, leaving you questioning what went wrong. However, there are several reasons why friendships lose momentum, and understanding these can help you navigate the emotions that arise.

1. **Life Gets in the Way**

Sometimes, friendships fade simply because of external circumstances. Perhaps you and your friend live far apart, or both of you are busy with young children, demanding careers, or other life commitments. It's important to recognize that these situations are not personal. When the opportunity arises to reconnect, avoid overanalysing the lapse. Instead, pick up where you left off and cherish the rekindled connection.

As Marcus Aurelius advises, "Do not waste what remains of your life in speculating about your neighbours, unless with a view to some mutual benefit" (Aurelius, trans. 2002).

Rather than dwelling on why the friendship drifted, focus on whether it can be revived in a meaningful way. True friendships can endure periods of dormancy and thrive again when given the chance.

2. **Hitting the Parameters of a Friendship**

In some cases, a friend may be unable to support you in a challenging situation. This could be due to their own limitations or fears, especially if the situation involves a toxic relationship or complex emotions. Reaching the natural limits of a friendship can feel hurtful, but it's essential to approach it with compassion. Recognize that not all friendships are equipped to handle every aspect of your life.

Epictetus reminds us: "If someone is unwilling to accept what is natural to their condition, do not try to compel them" (Epictetus, trans. 2008).

While this may seem harsh, it underscores the importance of respecting boundaries and focusing on relationships that can provide genuine support. Some friendships serve specific roles in our lives, and expecting them to fulfill all needs can lead to disappointment.

3. Processing and Moving On

When a friendship fades or falters, it's natural to feel a sense of loss. Reflect on the value the friendship brought to your life and honour the role it played. At the same time, accept that not all connections are meant to endure forever. The Stoics teach us to focus on what we can control and to let go of attachments that no longer serve us.

As Marcus Aurelius advises: "Receive without pride, let go without attachment" (Aurelius, trans. 2002).

By embracing this perspective, you can find peace and create space for new, meaningful connections. Instead of mourning what has passed, channel your energy into cultivating new relationships that align with your present values and circumstances.

Friendships, like all relationships, ebb and flow. Understanding the reasons behind the distance can help you navigate these transitions with grace and resilience, allowing you to cherish the bonds that remain and move forward with clarity.

Navigating the Loss of a Friendship: Breaking Up with Friends

While the end of a friendship may not carry the same societal weight as a romantic breakup, it can be just as emotionally impactful. Friendships often feel timeless, built on shared experiences, mutual support, and deep emotional bonds. When a friendship ends—whether due to conflict, distance, or simply growing apart—it can leave behind a profound sense of grief and confusion.

Understanding the Loss

The Stoics remind us that all relationships, even friendships, are transient. As Marcus Aurelius reflects: "Everything is ephemeral—both that which remembers and that which is remembered" (Aurelius, trans. 2002).

While this may seem unsettling, it invites us to appreciate friendships as they are rather than clinging to what they were or wishing they could last forever.

The end of a friendship often is not about failure but reflects the natural evolution of life. People grow, priorities shift, and what once connected us may no longer align. Accepting this impermanence does not diminish the friendship's value; rather, it honours its role in your life while making space for new connections.

Moving Forward with Stoic Resilience

The Stoics teach us to find strength in loss by focusing on what remains within our control. Losing a friendship does not negate its importance; rather, it underscores its impact on your life. As Seneca reminds us: "To bear trials with a calm mind robs misfortune of its strength and burden" (Seneca, trans. 1917).

By approaching the end of a friendship with reflection, acceptance, and gratitude, you can navigate the pain with grace and make room for new, meaningful connections. Instead of mourning what has passed, channel your energy into building relationships that align with your present values and growth.

Principles for Nurturing Healthy Friendships

Once you have recognized and let go of friendships that no longer serve you, the next step is to cultivate relationships that bring meaning and support to your life. The Stoics valued friendship not as a necessity but as a virtue—something that enhances life rather than completes it. True friendships are built on trust, mutual respect, and a shared commitment to growth and wisdom.

Consider these guiding principles as a foundation for fostering strong, enduring friendships:

1. Empathy

Deep, attentive listening strengthens the bonds of friendship. Instead of merely waiting for a turn to speak, true friends seek to understand each other's feelings and perspectives. Empathy does not mean agreeing with everything or enabling poor choices; rather, it is about offering support while maintaining personal integrity.

2. Presence

In a world filled with distractions, undivided attention is a rare and valuable gift. Being fully present—whether in moments of joy or hardship—demonstrates care and reinforces connection. When you make time for your friends, you show them that their experiences and emotions truly matter.

3. Honesty

Strong friendships thrive on authenticity and constructive honesty. Encouraging a friend's growth sometimes means offering difficult but necessary truths. As Seneca reminds us, "He who regards himself only, and enters into friendships for his own sake, reckons wrongly" (Seneca, trans. 1917).

Friendship is not a transaction but a mutual endeavour—one that flourishes through truthfulness and a willingness to help one another grow.

4. Vulnerability

True connection arises when we allow ourselves to be seen as we are. Being open and honest fosters deeper trust and understanding. The Stoics did not view vulnerability as weakness but as self-awareness and courage. A strong friendship provides a safe space for both people to express themselves without fear of judgment.

5. Mutual Support

A balanced friendship is a reciprocal exchange of care, encouragement, and trust. Being there for others is important, but so is recognizing when a friendship becomes one-sided. As Seneca wisely said, "The wise man is self-sufficient. Yet he desires friends, neighbours, and associates; for he is a social being by nature" (Seneca, trans. 1917).

Friendship is not about dependency but about shared enrichment. A fulfilling relationship is one where wisdom, joy, and support are exchanged freely, without obligation but with intention.

By embracing these principles, you can cultivate friendships that not only bring happiness but also encourage personal growth —relationships that exist not by chance, but by choice.

Final Reflections

Friendships are among life's most precious treasures. They shape our experiences, influence our growth, and provide comfort during life's challenges. Yet not all friendships are meant to last. The Stoic practice of *memento mori* reminds us that life is fleeting and that we should cherish the time we have with those who truly matter.

As Marcus Aurelius reflects, "Remember that you will die. Keep this thought at the forefront, and treat every interaction as though it could be the last" (Aurelius, trans. 2002).

This perspective does not encourage fear but rather mindfulness—an awareness that every moment with others is an opportunity to express kindness, gratitude, and sincerity.

As you reflect on the friendships in your life, ask yourself:

- Do these relationships uplift me or drain me?
- Are these friends trustworthy and loyal?
- Do they align with my values and encourage my growth?

Nurture the relationships that bring joy and meaning to your life, and do not be afraid to let go of those that no longer serve you. Life is too short for anything less.

By refining your friend filter, you create space for authentic, meaningful connections—relationships that reflect your values, enhance your well-being, and stand the test of time. And that is a gift worth treasuring.

4

RELATIVE CHAOS

FINDING SANITY AMID FAMILY DYSFUNCTION AND DISAGREEMENT

"Some things are up to us, and some things are not."

— EPICTETUS

FAMILY CAN BE both our greatest source of support and our greatest source of stress. One moment, we feel a deep sense of connection and belonging. The next, we are walking on eggshells, bracing for yet another argument, judgment, or misunderstanding.

Why does family sometimes feel like an emotional minefield? The answer lies not just in the dynamics we inherit but in our expectations of how family should function. We hope that parents will always understand us, that siblings will be lifelong allies, that holidays will bring warmth rather than tension. But as the Stoics remind us, expectations are often the root of suffering (Robertson, 2019).

We do not control the family we are born into. We cannot dictate their words, choices, or willingness to change. But we can control how we engage with them.

The Stoic Approach to Family Dynamics and Conflict

Stoicism offers a powerful framework for navigating family relationships without becoming consumed by them. By focusing on what is within our control, we can preserve our peace, set clear boundaries, and engage in ways that reflect our values (Pigliucci, 2017).

Three core Stoic principles help us reframe family dysfunction:

1. The Dichotomy of Control—Letting Go of Unrealistic Expectations

"Happiness and freedom begin with a clear understanding of one principle: some things are within our control, and some things are not" (Epictetus, trans. 2008, p. 11).

In family life, this means:

- You **cannot** control your relatives' opinions of you.
- You **cannot** force a toxic family member to change.
- You **cannot** erase past conflicts.

But you can control how you respond. Instead of arguing with reality, Stoicism teaches us to accept what is and focus on what we can actually change—our thoughts, actions, and emotional reactions (Robertson, 2019).

Practical Application:

The next time a family member criticizes you unfairly—whether it's about your career choices, parenting style, or life decisions—pause before reacting. Instead of immediately defending yourself or getting drawn into an argument, take a breath and ask yourself:

- *Am I in control of their perception?*

- *Or am I only in control of my response?*

Stoicism teaches us that we cannot dictate how others think or feel about us. Their opinions are shaped by their own experiences, biases, and expectations—things entirely beyond our control. However, we *do* have complete control over whether we let their words disrupt our inner peace.

Rather than reacting emotionally, consider responding with calm detachment and clarity. You might say:

- *"I appreciate your perspective, but I see things differently."*
- *"That's an interesting viewpoint. I'll give it some thought."*
- *"I understand that you feel strongly about this, but I'm comfortable with my decision."*

By responding in a measured way, you demonstrate emotional resilience and self-possession. More importantly, you protect your own well-being by refusing to be drawn into unnecessary conflict.

If the criticism continues, remember that silence is also a response. Walking away from an argument you didn't start—and don't need to finish—is an act of strength, not weakness. As Epictetus reminds us, "If someone succeeds in provoking you, realize that your mind is complicit in the provocation." You always have the power to disengage.

Over time, practising this kind of response will not only reduce stress but will also shift your family dynamics. When others see that their words no longer have the power to unsettle you, they may eventually stop trying. And even if they don't, you'll know that their opinions do not define your worth or your path.

2. *Amor Fati*—Embracing, Rather Than Resisting, Our Family Roles

Families shape us, for better or worse. Many of us are assigned roles early in life—the overachiever, the peacemaker, the rebel, the fixer. While these labels may feel restrictive, Stoicism teaches us to embrace our circumstances and use them as a path to growth (Robertson, 2019).

Practical Application:

If you feel stuck in a family role, begin by reflecting on how this role has shaped your experiences, both positively and negatively. *Amor Fati*, the Stoic principle of embracing one's fate, encourages us to see every challenge as an opportunity for growth.

1. **Identify the Role:** Start by acknowledging the role you've been assigned. Are you the problem-solver, always expected to mediate family conflicts? The responsible one, carrying the weight of others' expectations? Recognizing this pattern is the first step toward shifting it.
2. **Reframe the Narrative:** Instead of viewing your role as a burden, consider how it has built valuable strengths. For example:
    - If you've always been the *Scapegoat*, what skills have you developed in self-reliance and independent thinking?
    - If you're the *Caretaker*, how has this strengthened your emotional intelligence, and where might you need to establish healthier boundaries?
    - If you're the *Golden Child*, how can you learn to separate your worth from others' validation and define success on your own terms?
3. **Redefine Your Participation:** Ask yourself, *How can I engage differently?* If your role no longer serves you, shift your responses:
    - If you've always been the *Peacemaker*, practice saying, "I can't fix this for you."
    - If you're the *Fixer*, step back and allow others to take responsibility for their own problems.

    - If you're expected to be the *Responsible One*, recognize that your needs matter, too.
4. **Take Small, Intentional Steps:** Redefining your role doesn't mean an overnight transformation. It means making conscious choices—perhaps setting boundaries, stepping back from unnecessary conflict, or asserting your independence in small but meaningful ways.

By learning to apply *Amor Fati,* you shift from frustration to empowerment. Rather than feeling trapped by your family role, you can use it as a foundation for personal growth. Instead of resisting the past, embrace what it has taught you and move forward with intention.

3. Setting Boundaries Without Guilt—Protecting Your Peace

Setting boundaries reinforces our autonomy and aligns with Stoic philosophy, primarily through the principles of control, self-discipline, and inner tranquillity. Stoicism teaches that while we cannot control how others behave, we can control how we engage with them. Boundaries are an expression of this control—an assertion of what we will and will not allow into our lives. Boundaries also allow us to choose when to engage and when to disengage.

Boundaries are not about controlling others, but about defining how we engage with them. A common mistake is believing that setting a boundary requires others to agree with or respect it (Brown, 2018).

But a boundary is an action, not a request.

- You cannot control whether a parent stops criticizing you.
- But you can choose to disengage when the criticism begins.

- You cannot control whether a toxic sibling stops guilt-tripping you.
- But you can refuse to engage in conversations that centre on guilt.

In other words, we don't have to take the bait. And yet, some family members will test boundaries not because they don't understand them, but because they view these interactions as a game—one where they win if they get a reaction. This is particularly true in dysfunctional dynamics where manipulation, guilt, or control are used to maintain power. The moment you engage in the argument, justify yourself, or try to prove your point, you've been drawn into their frame.

Practical Application

Instead of debating your boundaries, enforce them with calm consistency.

- If a conversation turns critical, don't argue—simply disengage:
- *"I won't continue this conversation if it turns negative."* Then, physically remove yourself if necessary.
- If a relative repeatedly ignores your limits, respond with quiet firmness rather than defensiveness:
- *"I've already said where I stand on this, and I'm not going to discuss it further."*
- If someone deliberately escalates to provoke a reaction, resist the urge to explain or defend yourself. Instead, use silence as your strongest tool. Without engagement, the "game" loses its power.

The key is follow-through. Boundaries that aren't enforced consistently become meaningless, and some people will test them repeatedly just to see if they can wear you down. Stoicism teaches us that true control lies in how we respond—not in changing the behaviour of others, but in ensuring we remain steady, unshaken, and at peace.

Putting the Three Stoic Principles into Practice:

The three principles—letting go of unrealistic expectations, *Amor fati,* and setting boundaries—provide a practical framework for handling difficult family conflicts. Here are three examples of how they can be applied to real-life situations.

Handling Family Criticism with Calmness

Imagine a parent or sibling constantly judging your life choices. The instinctive reaction might be to defend yourself, argue, or feel frustrated. But Stoicism teaches that we cannot control others' opinions—only our response to them.

Instead of engaging in a battle of words, remind yourself, *"Their judgment is about them, not me."* Respond with calm detachment. A simple phrase like, *"I hear you, but I see things differently,"* acknowledges their perspective without inviting conflict.

Dealing with Manipulation or Emotional Guilt

Some relatives use guilt to influence or control our decisions. This can lead to resentment or a sense of obligation. Stoicism reminds us that guilt-tripping is their issue, not ours. Marcus Aurelius put it clearly, "You have power over your mind—not outside events. Realize this, and you will find strength."

If you're being pressured into something you don't want to do, respond firmly but without hostility. "I won't be attending, but I hope you enjoy." No justification is needed.

Managing Toxic Family Relationships

When a relationship is chronically draining. Stoicism suggests that instead of trying to fix the person, we focus on what is within our control—our own actions and boundaries.

Rather than feeling responsible for their behaviour, accept that change is not within your power. Set limits on engagement, and if necessary, step away with grace rather than resentment.

Seneca reminds us, "You are the product of your own thoughts, not of others' opinions."

You are not obligated to maintain relationships that are consistently harmful.

Embracing Stoicism in Family Life

Family conflict is inevitable. But suffering is optional. Stoicism does not ask us to ignore pain, tolerate dysfunction, or suppress our emotions. Instead, it provides a framework for engaging with family dynamics from a place of wisdom, acceptance, and resilience. The philosophy teaches that by focusing on what is within our control, embracing challenges as opportunities for growth, and refusing to engage in unnecessary battles, we can cultivate inner stability—even amid the most chaotic relationships.

Consider these reflective questions:

- What family expectations am I holding onto that no longer serve me?
- Where can I set boundaries that protect my well-being without guilt?
- How can I approach difficult interactions with calmness rather than reactivity?

The principles discussed so far provide a broad foundation for managing family dynamics through a Stoic lens. But how does this philosophy apply to the specific challenges of modern family life? Can a philosophy from ancient Rome help navigate the complexities of blended families, co-parenting, or the pressures of raising children in a digital world?

The answer is yes—because while family structures have evolved, the fundamental pressures of family life remain timeless. The weight of expectations, the emotional complexities of relationships, and the need for resilience in the face of uncertainty have always been part of the human experience.

The Manufactured Pressures of Modern Family Life

The pressure to "get it right" as a parent, stepparent, or partner is not only overwhelming—it is deliberately cultivated. Entire industries, worth billions, profit from our fears:

- The fear of not feeding children the "right" foods.
- The fear of not providing enough in terms of material goods and opportunities.
- The fear of not spending enough "quality time," even as social media distorts what that should look like.

Blended families face additional complexities. Stepparents navigate evolving roles and external judgments. Co-parents balance shifting schedules, differing household rules, and conflicting parenting styles. Meanwhile, teenagers are subjected to relentless social pressures, the illusion of curated perfection, and the expectation of effortless success.

So, how can Stoicism provide a path to peace amid this chaos?

The answer lies in its core teachings:

- Focus on what is within your control.
- Embrace the present without resistance.
- Gradually let go of external expectations.

In the following three sections, we will explore how these Stoic principles can be applied to modern family dynamics—offering practical strategies for navigating challenges with clarity, resilience, and peace.

Part 1: Breaking Free from Manufactured Chaos

In today's world, family life is often shaped by external pressures rather than personal values. Industries, marketing strategies, and social expectations create a constant sense of inadequacy, making it difficult to feel we are ever doing enough.

The Stoics remind us that many of these pressures are artificial—they are external forces that do not define our happiness or self-worth. By recognizing what is truly within our control, we can liberate ourselves from the cycle of perfectionism, guilt, and comparison.

Three major forces drive modern parental anxiety: food culture, consumer industries, and social media.

1. The Food Industry Trap: Unrealistic Standards and Manufactured Guilt

Food has become a battleground, where families are caught in a no-win cycle—not just feeding their children but navigating judgment, marketing tactics, and impossible standards.

Families face criticism from every angle:

- Processed snacks? Labelled as unhealthy or lazy.
- Perfectly curated organic meals? Considered over-the-top or privileged.

But this isn't really about food—it's about control. It reflects a culture obsessed with evaluating family choices, making parents feel inadequate no matter what they do (Gillis, 2023).

Adding to this is pester power—billions spent by food companies to bypass parental judgment and directly target children through bright packaging, cartoon mascots, and strategic placement (Market Research Future, 2023).

Marcus Aurelius reminds us: "Do what you can, with what you have, where you are" (Aurelius, trans. 2002).

Rather than chasing an unattainable standard, focus on what is practical. Instead of striving for perfection, prioritize what is sustainable.

- Let go of guilt for choosing convenience when necessary.
- Teach children about balance rather than restriction.
- Reject external judgment in favour of what works for your family.

Sometimes good enough is good enough.

2. Manufacturing the Need for Products: The Business of Parental Insecurity

Industries thrive on parental self-doubt, selling solutions for every perceived shortcoming—from developmental toys to expert-endorsed parenting courses.

While many products are beneficial, it is the relentless messaging that fuels the fear of failure. Families are constantly made to feel that they:

- Need to buy more to ensure their child's success.
- Must upgrade constantly to keep up with "better" parenting methods.
- Are falling behind if they don't have the latest educational tools.

The baby care products market alone was valued at over $19 billion in 2023—a testament to how deeply commercial interests shape modern parenting (Market Research Future, 2023).

Epictetus reminds us, "Wealth consists not in having great possessions, but in having few wants" (Epictetus, trans. 2008).

Before buying into the latest trend, ask:

- Is this truly necessary, or just marketed as necessary?
- Will this improve my child's well-being, or just my sense of keeping up?

This does not mean rejecting every tool, toy, or convenience—it means letting go of guilt and focusing on what truly serves your family.

3. Social Media and the Illusion of Perfect Families

While social media has transformed family connectivity, it has also fuelled unrealistic expectations—dictating self-worth, influencing parenting decisions, and promoting a culture of comparison.

Social media is not inherently harmful, but when the curated digital world dictates real-life choices, it creates unnecessary stress.

The Illusion of Perfection: How Social Media Warps Reality

Social media thrives on curation—spotless homes, beautifully plated meals, and well-behaved children enjoying the ultimate family day out (Gillis, 2023).

For teenagers, it is particularly tough and manifests in the illusion of effortless academic success and flawless social lives and pressure to constantly optimize, achieve, and curate their identity.

Algorithm-driven content amplifies this anxiety—promoting educational tools, beauty filters, and social validation strategies that create an endless cycle of consumption and self-doubt (Robertson, 2019).

Seneca warned, "You are your own worst enemy if you are always looking at others" *(Seneca, trans. 1997).*

Instead of comparing, ask yourself:

- Am I making this choice for my family or for external validation?
- Would I still value this experience if no one saw it?

The best moments within a family are often not curated but unplanned.

4. Shared Custody and the Pressure to "Make Up for Lost Time"

For separated families, the pressure to maximize quality time can become overwhelming. Parents feel pressured by external forces to compensate for time apart by planning elaborate experiences, buying gifts, or making every moment count.

But the pursuit of perfect moments often steals the joy from them. Real connection isn't built through grand gestures—it's built through:

- Consistency over performance.
- Presence over perfection.
- Authentic attention over curated experiences.

5. The Reality of Co-Parenting: Beyond the Highlight Reel

Social media often romanticizes co-parenting, presenting an idealized version where:

- Parents effortlessly coordinate schedules.
- Communication is seamless and harmonious.
- There is never conflict, resentment, or struggle.

But in reality, co-parenting often involves:

- **Logistical chaos**—the never-ending suitcase relay, lost shoes, and schedule confusion.

- **Parenting style clashes**—where some differences cannot be reconciled.
- **Letting go of control**—accepting that the other parent will do things their own way.

Epictetus reminds us: "Don't demand that things happen as you wish, but wish that they happen as they do happen" (Epictetus, trans. 2008). Co-parenting doesn't have to be about achieving perfection—it's about working with reality, not against it.

Shifting to this perspective takes time but allows for:

- More peace and less frustration.
- Healthier boundaries and fewer battles.
- A focus on what can be controlled, rather than dwelling on what cannot.

The modern family experience is burdened by external expectations—from industries, media, and cultural norms that fuel unnecessary pressure. But family life is not a performance.

By embracing practicality over perfection, connection over comparison, and presence over pressure, you can start to reclaim family life on your own terms.

Part 2: Stoicism for Blended Families

Blended families bring unique joys and unexpected challenges. There is no singular "right way" to merge different histories, parenting styles, and expectations. Some of these challenges may include:

1. **Loyalty Conflicts** – A stepchild may feel torn between their biological parent and stepparent. For example, they might hesitate to form a close bond with their

stepparent out of fear that their biological parent will feel replaced or hurt (Papernow, 2013).

2. **Parenting Disagreements** – A stepparent may favour strict discipline, while the biological parent adopts a more lenient approach. These differences can create tension, leaving the child caught between competing parenting styles (Hetherington & Clingempeel, 1992).
3. **Stepsibling Rivalry** – Differences in parental attention or resources can lead to jealousy or exclusion. One sibling may feel overlooked if their stepsibling receives more praise or privileges (Gillis, 2023).
4. **Extended Family Tensions** – A grandparent from the biological side may struggle to accept stepchildren, subtly favouring their biological grandchildren in ways that create division (Minuchin, 1974).

But Stoicism offers practical tools to navigate this unpredictability with grace, patience, and resilience.

Rather than striving for flawless harmony, Stoic principles encourage acceptance, adaptability, and emotional clarity—allowing families to coexist with stability rather than perfection.

1. Accepting What You Can't Control — *Amor Fati*

Stepparents often struggle with feeling like an outsider. Co-parents wrestle with different rules in different households. Children navigate loyalties and shifting family dynamics.

The Stoic approach? Acceptance. Rather than resisting the challenges, Stoicism teaches us to embrace them as part of the journey.

Instead of dwelling on what feels unfair or frustrating, focus on what is within your control:

- The environment you create in your own home.
- The way you model patience and consistency.

- The respect you show to differing parenting styles—even when you disagree.

Whenever frustration arises, pause and reframe the situation:

- Am I resisting what I cannot change?
- What is within my power to influence?
- How can I respond with calm acceptance rather than emotional reaction?

Blended families are not about controlling outcomes—they are about adapting to reality with wisdom and resilience.

2. Boundaries Without Guilt — Practicing Discernment

Stepparents often feel caught between engagement and overstepping.

- Too involved? You risk resentment.
- Too distant? You risk detachment.

The key to navigating this balance? Boundaries. Boundaries are not rejection—they are clarity. They define what is within your role and what is not. Marcus Aurelius reminds us, "If you seek tranquillity, do less. Or, more accurately, do what's essential" (Aurelius, trans. 2002).

Before stepping into a conflict, decision, or family tension, ask:

- Is this truly my role to step into?
- Am I acting out of guilt, or out of intention?
- Would engaging in this situation align with my values—or just my emotions?

Boundaries protect relationships by ensuring that each family member understands their role, autonomy, and emotional space.

Instead of forcing closeness, let relationships develop naturally —built on trust rather than obligation.

3. Letting Go of the "Perfect Family" Ideal

Many blended families feel pressure to function like a traditional nuclear family.

- Are we "blended" enough?
- Should we feel more like a "real" family?
- Why do other families seem to have it all together?

But there is no universal definition of "normal." Every family —blended, extended, or nuclear—has its own rhythms, challenges, and strengths.

The goal is not to blend seamlessly. The goal is to coexist peacefully.

Seneca reminds us, "Comparison is a thief of peace" (Seneca, trans. 1997).

Instead of thinking: *"Why isn't our family more like...?"*

Reframe the question: *"What's unique about what we are building?"*

Blended families do not have to look a certain way to be meaningful.

- A peaceful home is enough.
- Respectful co-parenting is enough.
- Strong individual relationships are enough.

Let go of the external narrative of what family "should" look like—and embrace what it is.

Blended families are not about perfection—they are about presence.

The Stoics remind us that challenges are inevitable—but how we respond to them is our choice.

By focusing on:

- Acceptance rather than resistance *(Amor Fati).*
- Boundaries rather than overextension *(Discernment).*
- Peace over comparison *(Letting go of idealized images).*

Blended families can build strong, healthy relationships—not by forcing unity, but by allowing connection to grow naturally.

Part 3: The Cost of Exclusion—When Families Can't Keep Up

For families unable to afford the ever-growing list of must-have products, educational tools, and social trends, the impact extends beyond missing out on luxuries. It creates stress, exclusion, and even shame.

Social media fuels the illusion that good parenting, academic success, and social belonging are tied to what can be bought. When parents can't provide the latest baby gadget, when students lack access to high-end tutoring apps or fashionable outfits, it can feel as though they're falling behind before they've even started.

The Emotional and Financial Toll on Parents

This pressure weighs heavily on parents, who may feel guilt or anxiety over their inability to provide what social media deems essential. Some even stretch their finances to breaking point just to prevent their child from feeling left out. The Stoics teach that control lies in our choices, not external pressures.

But for families, these outside events—exclusion, financial pressure, and the heartbreak of watching their child struggle—feel deeply personal. Research indicates that the pressure to provide materially for children—whether through extracurriculars, technology, or social experiences—can lead to heightened parental stress and financial overextension (Luthar et al., 2019; Twenge, 2017).

Yet, the Stoics remind us that much of this suffering is not caused by our circumstances, but by our perception of them.

Seneca wrote, “It is not the man who has too little, but the man who craves more, who is poor” (Seneca, 1997).

By shifting focus from what we lack to what we already have, we regain control over our emotional responses. Parents may not be able to shield their children from every disappointment, but they can teach them to value connection over consumption, resilience over status, and self-worth over social comparison.

A System Designed to Widen the Gap

The push for constant consumption doesn’t just widen financial gaps—it deepens cycles of inequality, making those without privilege feel that success, happiness, and even basic social inclusion are out of reach. The Stoics caution against defining our worth by external standards, reminding us that wealth is not about possessions, but about perspective.

Instead of measuring success by external markers, Stoicism invites us to redefine it based on presence, values, and resilience. The latest gadgets, the curated experiences, and the ever-expanding list of “must-haves” are distractions from what truly matters: the ability to find contentment within.

For families, this means learning to let go of guilt over what they cannot provide and instead focusing on what they can—unwavering support, love, and a sense of stability that no material possession can replace.

Final Thoughts: Family Life on Your Own Terms — *The Dolce Far Niente* Approach

Family life—whether traditional, blended, or co-parenting—is never perfect. But Stoicism provides a way to engage with it without being consumed by it.

- Say no when it matters. *(Discernment)*
- Let go of judgment. *(Mastering indifference)*
- Choose flexibility over rigidity. *(Amor fati)*

- Prioritize connection over performance. *(Living with presence)*

The Power of *Dolce Far Niente*: The Sweetness of Doing Nothing

The modern world glorifies optimization, efficiency, and constant improvement. But in Italy, they embrace something different—*Dolce Far Niente*, the sweetness of doing nothing.

This philosophy is not about laziness but about learning to savour life instead of filling it with artificial urgency. It is a reminder that we don't always have to be productive to be present.

Instead of constantly planning, fixing, and managing family life, allow space for:

- **Unstructured time**—letting go of the need to schedule every moment.
- **Simple joy in shared meals**—without rushing to the next thing.
- **Being together without an agenda**—because connection happens in stillness, too.

Let go of manufactured pressure. Embrace imperfection. Find joy in what already is.

And add a generous dash of *Dolce Far Niente* to life!

5

REBUILDING AFTER A BREAKUP

A STOIC APPROACH TO RENEWAL

"Accept the things to which fate binds you and love the people with whom fate brings you together but do so with all your heart."

— MARCUS AURELIUS

THE END of a relationship can feel like the closing of a chapter that shaped who you were, what you believed, and what you thought you could depend on. In a world that often measures the success of relationships by their duration, it is easy to feel like you have failed. But does longevity truly define success? Perhaps success in relationships should be measured instead by growth, understanding, and shared experiences. What if a relationship's true value lies in how it shapes and transforms us, even when it ends? Sometimes, the end of a relationship signals personal growth—what once fit your life may no longer align with who you have become. This is not failure; it is a sign of change and evolution.

Breakups often stem from a period of significant compromise. While compromise is an inevitable part of any relationship, it becomes problematic when it requires suppressing core values, neglecting personal needs, or diminishing vital aspects of oneself to maintain the status quo. Over time, this erosion of authenticity can signal that a relationship has reached its natural limit. The Stoics teach that one should act in alignment with virtue and reason rather than attachment or fear (Epictetus, *Discourses*, 2.2). If maintaining a relationship means betraying one's values or sacrificing well-being, then its dissolution is not failure but an act of self-honesty and growth.

Whether to leave is a difficult question and arriving at answers can be deeply personal and challenging. The Stoic wisdom of acceptance lies not in clinging to what feels comfortable or familiar but in courageously acknowledging when a meaningful chapter has come to its conclusion. If you are grappling with the decision to leave, you are not alone—there are many resources available to guide you through that process. While this chapter will not focus on the decision itself, it will explore how Stoicism—through its teachings on acceptance, resilience, and emotional control—can help you heal and rebuild after a relationship ends.

Ending or accepting the end of a relationship takes strength, and it is almost always painful, often accompanied by feelings of regret. During this transition, pain can also be unintentionally invalidated by others who try to comfort with statements such as, "You'll get over it," or "Forget them, you'll soon meet someone else." Healing takes time, and no one should expect themselves to "move on" before they are ready. In this context, healing involves allowing oneself to fully experience and process emotions without judgment, an approach that aligns with the Stoic practice of self-examination (*Meditations*, 4.3).

As you process grief, it is important to recognize that the heartache of a breakup activates the same areas of the brain involved in physical pain (Verhallen et al., 2019). This intense response can feel overwhelming, a stark reminder of how deeply you were attached. However, this pain also holds meaning—it is a testament to the capacity to love deeply and fully. If you have loved once, you can love again. The loss may feel consuming now, but it also shows that you are capable of building meaningful connections in the future. This perspective may feel of little comfort initially but can be a source of hope as healing progresses.

The end of a relationship is not a failure; it is a natural part of life's flow. The opening quote, in the context of a breakup, reminds us that while it is important to love fully in the moment, relationships are shaped by fate and impermanence. By embracing this impermanence, we honour the love shared while letting go with grace, trusting that endings create space for personal growth and new beginnings (*Meditations*, 5.8). This perspective lays the foundation for healing and fostering healthier, more fulfilling connections in the future.

The End of a Relationship as a Positive Turning Point

Relationships, whether toxic or non-toxic, are an integral part of our lives, shaping who we are and how we grow. When they end, the impact is profound, and the healing process is deeply personal. The lessons we take from these endings vary depending on the dynamics of the relationship. Toxic relationships, for example, often demand a focus on breaking free and reclaiming oneself, while non-toxic breakups require letting go with grace and honouring the love that once was.

This section explores both scenarios, recognizing that every ending—no matter the circumstances—carries an opportunity for transformation. By examining the unique challenges and lessons of toxic and non-toxic breakups, we can approach these experiences with greater clarity, compassion, and resilience. Stoicism provides a framework to navigate the pain, empowering us to view endings not as failures, but as turning points for growth and renewal.

1. Toxic Relationships: Breaking Free with Courage and Wisdom

Recognizing that you are in a toxic relationship is often the first step toward reclaiming your sense of self.

Often, cold formative relationships can lead to an attraction to narcissists because of their initial charisma and warmth, but this comfort is only temporary. Early emotional neglect can make the exaggerated affection of narcissists seem appealing, creating a cycle of attachment that ultimately leads to disappointment (Durvasula, 2019). Stoicism teaches us to recognize these patterns and detach from false hopes, allowing reason and self-awareness to guide our choices (Epictetus, *Discourses*).

However, identifying the subtle yet destructive dynamics at play—like manipulation, gaslighting, or emotional neglect—can feel confusing and isolating. The work of Dr. Ramani Durvasula and Rebecca Zung provides invaluable insights into narcissistic behaviour and toxic relationship patterns (Durvasula, 2019; Zung, 2020). While not all toxic relationships involve narcissists, many exhibit narcissistic traits, making it essential to examine these patterns and cycles.

The four pillars of narcissism—a lack of empathy, grandiosity, chronic entitlement, and an ongoing need for admiration—help explain the driving forces behind many toxic relationships (Durvasula, 2019). Narcissists are often charming and charismatic, using these traits to manipulate others for their own benefit. Toxic relationships involving narcissists often follow distinct patterns, including:

- **Love-bombing** – An overwhelming display of affection to gain control.
- **Devaluation** – Gaslighting, belittling, and manipulation.
- **Discardment** – Emotional abandonment once their needs are no longer being met.

Understanding these patterns can bring clarity to the confusion of a toxic relationship. Narcissists often employ tactics like:

- **Future faking** – Making empty promises of a better future to keep you invested.
- **Breadcrumbing** – Offering minimal attention to maintain control.
- **Hollow promises of change** – Temporary improvements that lack sincerity.

These tactics foster emotional dependency while eroding self-esteem. Many victims of such relationships hold onto the hope that the "better version" of their partner will emerge, further reinforcing the cycle of abuse.

The Stoics teach us to focus on what lies within our control. Recognizing the dynamics at play allows you to step back, reassess your needs, and prioritize self-discovery.

Breaking Free: Radical Acceptance and Practical Strategies

Two critical concepts can help break free from the emotional grip of a toxic relationship: Radical Acceptance and rejecting the Sunk Cost Fallacy.

1. **Radical Acceptance:** This involves acknowledging the reality of the relationship as it is, not as you wish it to be. Narcissists are often incapable of meeting your emotional needs. Radical acceptance doesn't condone their behaviour but helps you let go of the futile hope that they will change. As the Stoics advise, "Do not wish for things to be other than they are" (Epictetus, *Discourses*, 1.6). This mindset allows you to detach emotionally and move forward.

Example: You might accept that waiting for your partner to become the person you wanted is futile: this can free you from the cycle of disappointment and false hope.

2. **Rejecting the Sunk Cost Fallacy:** The sunk cost fallacy is the idea that because you've invested so much time, energy, or love into a relationship, you feel compelled to stay and make it work, even when it is no longer serving you. (Stanovich, 2013). This thinking can trap you in harmful situations, as you focus on past investments rather than current realities or future possibilities. Realizing that staying will only lead to further harm can be liberating. Letting go of what you've already invested allows you to focus on building a healthier future, prioritizing your well-being over the weight of the past.

Using the DEEP Strategy

Dr. Ramani Durvasula's DEEP Strategy offers an invaluable framework for detaching emotionally and navigating interactions with a toxic partner (Durvasula, 2019). These principles align closely with Stoic teachings on controlling one's reactions:

1. **Don't Defend:** Defending oneself against baseless accusations only fuels the narcissist's desire for control. Instead, choosing silence or a calm acknowledgment without justification can prevent further escalation. Defending one's position when words are repeatedly twisted only serves to empower the narcissist. Choosing not to engage removes fuel from the fire.
2. **Don't Engage:** Engaging in arguments or trying to get a narcissist to see reason often drains energy and escalates conflict. Disengaging, both physically and emotionally, is often the only way to maintain one's sanity and protect emotional well-being.
3. **Don't Explain:** Explaining feelings or decisions rarely leads to understanding in these relationships and often invites further manipulation. Recognizing that repeated explanations only lead to frustration and

conflict allows one to step back and preserve their peace of mind.

4. **Don't Personalize:** Narcissists' attacks reflect their own insecurities, not the worth of the person being attacked. Recognizing this creates emotional distance. It's also important not to make personal comments about their behaviour as this can provoke rage. Understanding that their cruelty stems from a need for control, and not from a reflection of one's own value, allows individuals to stop taking their insults personally.

By applying these principles, you can gradually break free from the emotional chains of the relationship detach from the narcissist's energy, stop fighting battles that are not yours to fight, and reclaim your sense of self and emotional freedom.

A Stoic Lens on Healing and Growth

The Stoics remind us to embrace every experience, even painful ones, as opportunities for growth. As Seneca said, "Every new beginning comes from some other beginning's end" (*Letters to Lucilius*, 71.17). Leaving a toxic relationship is not a failure but a courageous step toward healing and rediscovery. The principle of *Amor Fati*—the love of fate—encourages us to see even the most difficult moments as necessary parts of our journey. As you heal, you may come to realize that *your pain becomes your medicine* (wise words that somebody once said to me.) The suffering endured in a toxic relationship is not meaningless; it teaches resilience, self-awareness, and the strength to set boundaries. By reframing the pain as a transformative force, you can emerge from the experience with renewed clarity and purpose. In this way, the end of a toxic relationship becomes a catalyst for rebuilding yourself and your life.

2. Non-Toxic Relationships: Letting Go with Grace

Not all relationships end in toxicity; some simply run their course as people grow in different directions. These relationships, built on mutual respect and care, can end for many reasons—distance, changing life priorities, or irreconcilable differences. While less dramatic than toxic breakups, these endings still carry profound emotions and challenges.

The Stoics remind us to embrace impermanence as a natural part of life. As Marcus Aurelius reflects, "Anything that happens has happened rightly. Look closely and you will see this" (*Meditations*, 4.10). Even when a relationship ends, it is not necessarily a mistake or a failure; some, however beautiful they once were, are not meant to last forever. Instead of mourning their end as a failure, we can view them as chapters in our journey that have shaped who we are.

The end of a non-toxic relationship requires reflection, gratitude, and acceptance. Consider the lessons it offered—perhaps it taught you about love, compromise, or communication. Maybe it challenged you to grow in ways you hadn't anticipated. Gratitude for these moments allows you to release the relationship with grace, focusing not on the loss but on how it enriched your life.

As Marcus Aurelius reminds us, "Dwell on the beauty of life. Watch the stars and see yourself running with them" (*Meditations*, 7.47). The love shared in a non-toxic relationship is never wasted—it becomes a part of who you are, reminding you of life's richness and your capacity for meaningful connection.

Letting go doesn't diminish the relationship's significance; it honours its role in your life. Trusting that every relationship serves its purpose can help you move forward with a sense of peace and renewal. Stoicism teaches us that life's transitions are opportunities to grow, not reasons to despair.

The Power of Mental Escape: Freeing Yourself When Leaving Isn't an Option

Leaving a relationship may seem like the obvious solution, but it's not always possible. For many, the decision to stay in an unhealthy relationship is rooted in financial dependence, a lack of support networks, or concerns about the well-being of children. These are valid concerns, and it's important to recognize that, in some cases, physically leaving may not be feasible in the short term, if at all.

Sometimes, practical barriers, emotional entanglements, and a lack of readiness all play a part in hindering that process. While you may not be able to leave right away, you don't have to remain emotionally trapped.

Even when physical separation isn't an option, you are not powerless. One of the most empowering principles you can adopt is mental detachment, a key concept in Stoicism. While you cannot always control external circumstances, you can control how you respond to them. As Epictetus reminds us, "It's not what happens to you, but how you react to it that matters" (*Discourses*, I.I). This wisdom underscores the power of emotional detachment in even the most challenging circumstances

Mental detachment takes time and effort. It's not about suppressing emotions but learning to navigate them intentionally. For example, this might mean recognizing your partner's manipulations for what they are and reframing your emotional responses: Remind yourself that their words are about controlling you, not a reflection of your worth. Over time, you may find that you can detach from the constant drama, even though you are still physically in the relationship.

Radical acceptance also plays a critical role. Rather than wishing for things to be different or ruminating on how unfair the situation is, you accept the reality of your circumstances as they are. This isn't resignation; it's a way of clearing your mind to think clearly, act strategically, and plan the next steps. The ability to shift focus from what is outside our control to what is within it is central to Stoic resilience.

Seneca also reinforces this principle, reminding us that while suffering exists, our interpretation of it determines its effect on us. He states, "We suffer more in imagination than in reality" (*Letters to Lucilius*, 13.4). Applying this perspective to an unhealthy relationship means recognizing that much of our emotional pain stems from fear of change, uncertainty, or self-doubt rather than the reality of the situation itself. When we learn to control our perception, we regain power over our emotional world.

This process might allow you to reclaim your sense of self long before you physically leave and empowering you to leave on your terms—for example, waiting until you are financially stable, emotionally ready, and have a plan in place to move forward confidently.

Moving Forward: What the Stoics Can Teach Us About Emotional Triggers

Breakups can be rife with emotional triggers that hinder the healing process. For instance:

- Seeing someone you once loved—and may still care for —struggle or appear unhappy can stir up complex emotions, particularly if you were the one to initiate the breakup. It's natural to feel a lingering sense of connection to their well-being, but it's essential to recognize that their happiness or suffering is no longer your responsibility. While compassion is a natural response, you cannot control their emotional state. Your focus should remain on your own healing and personal growth.

You left for a reason, likely after a long and thoughtful journey. Remind yourself of those reasons and stay grounded in your decision. Allowing yourself to be manipulated by guilt or misplaced responsibility will only hinder the progress you've made. Prioritize your well-being and trust that letting go is an act of care for both you and them.

- Feeling that one person is the sole source of your happiness can lead to a sense of entitlement toward the person or the relationship even after it has ended. This mindset often results in anger and frustration, particularly when betrayal occurs, or they move on to start a new life. In these moments, the wisdom of Lao Tzu offers comfort: "When I let go of what I am, I become what I might be" (*Tao Te Ching*, Chapter 44).

By embracing the transformative power of letting go, we can see a breakup as part of life's natural flow rather than a loss. This shift in perspective allows us to release resentment, grow from the experience, and move toward a brighter future.

- Seeing an ex begin a new chapter in their life can be challenging, stirring feelings of jealousy and inadequacy, especially if you're currently alone. However, Epictetus reminds us: "Never depend on the admiration of others. There is no strength in it. Personal merit cannot be derived from an external source" (*Discourses*, 1.3). This wisdom highlights the importance of recognizing that our worth is not dictated by how others perceive us, nor should it hinge on comparisons to someone else's life. Instead, true strength emerges when we focus on our own journey, growth, and self-discovery, independent of external validation.

- The belief that *"I'll never get over this person"* can deepen despair and prolong suffering. Stoicism reminds us that all things, including pain, are temporary. Marcus Aurelius teaches us that time and change are constant forces, and this moment of heartbreak will eventually

> pass. As Seneca wisely counselled, "Don't rush the process. It's okay to feel the pain and let it fade in its own time" (*Letters to Lucilius*, 13.6)

By embracing patience and allowing yourself to fully experience the emotions, you can gradually heal and move forward, trusting that every wound softens with time.

Self-Compassion in the Healing Process

Navigating the end of a relationship is incredibly difficult, and it would be idealistic to expect ourselves to remain stoical throughout the entire process. There will be times when emotions overwhelm you, and you lose sight of the bigger picture. To this end, Marcus Aurelius's advice on gentle persistence and self-compassion serves as a soothing reminder, "If you are unable to do what you have in mind, then do what you are able to do. And do it with all the power you have. But be gentle with yourself and continue to work on it."

6

LIFE AFTER LOSS

NAVIGATING GRIEF AND HONOURING

GRIEF IS AN UNWELCOME VISITOR, arriving unbidden and unrelenting. It reshapes the fabric of our lives, casting long shadows over everything we thought we knew. While deeply personal and unique, grief also unites us in its raw humanity, reminding us of our shared vulnerability and resilience.

This chapter does not seek to diminish the profound pain of loss or offer empty platitudes. Instead, it delves into the essence of grief: how it challenges us, reshapes us, and ultimately shows us a way forward.

How Grief Is Shaped by Loss

The worst day of my life, which I alluded to in the Preface, was the day the police knocked on my door to tell me my husband had been killed by a drunk driver. In that instant, my world was irreparably changed. The pain was unimaginable, and healing was —and in some ways still is—gradual. Yet, as time passed, I began to see how that loss reshaped me in ways I could never have foreseen.

Grief is deeply personal, taking on many forms depending on the nature of the loss. My experience taught me that, while the pain of loss is universal, the way we navigate its aftermath is profoundly individual. For instance:

- Sudden loss might leave us grappling with shock and a sense of injustice, especially if it involves a perpetrator, as we struggle with feelings of anger and the need for accountability.
- Suicide can evoke a complex mix of guilt, anger, and unanswerable questions, as we wonder what signs we missed or what we could have done differently.
- When a loved one dies of old age, grief often takes the form of honouring a life well-lived and finding peace in their natural and gentle passing, despite missing them deeply.
- The death of a child strikes at the very foundation of our being—a loss so untimely and profound that it can challenge the core of intimate relationships, as we're forced to reckon with a reality where parents should not outlive their children.
- Loss through a long illness, such as dementia or cancer, may bring a mix of relief and sorrow; we might grieve the person we lost long before their death while finding comfort in their release from suffering.

Each of these experiences presents unique emotional challenges, yet all grief shares a common thread: it demands to be felt before it can be integrated into our lives.

The Messy Reality of Grief

Grief is not a tidy process. It does not follow a straight path, nor does it adhere to a predictable timeline. The widely known five stages of grief—denial, anger, bargaining, depression, and acceptance—first proposed by Elisabeth Kübler-Ross (2005), serve more as a framework than a rulebook. These "textbook" stages often fail to capture the full range of emotions and experiences that accompany grief. These stages can overlap, recur, or be skipped entirely. You might feel calm one day and shattered the next. This is normal.

In the immediate aftermath of my husband's death, I felt numb. In utter disbelief, I drifted through those first days, unable to fully process what had happened. It was Christmas, yet I have no real memory of what I did or how I coped. That blankness, that haze—it was as much a part of my grieving as the sadness that followed.

Rather than treating grief as a series of steps to complete, it is more helpful to think of it as a nonlinear process—one filled with spirals, detours, and moments of stillness. Grief does not need to be solved; it needs to be lived through. Though it felt counterintuitive amid the chaos of grief, I now know that caring for myself was essential to begin healing. Sometimes, grief is so profound that it shatters the foundations of our lives, leaving us unsure of how to move forward. In these moments, all we can do is focus on small steps—one day, or even one hour, at a time.

As Marcus Aurelius wisely observed, "Don't let your imagination be crushed by life as a whole. Stick with the situation at hand" *(*Meditations, *8.36).* This insight encourages us to shift our focus away from overwhelming emotions and instead deal with grief in manageable moments. It is a reminder that, however chaotic grief may feel, we are always capable of taking the next small step.

However we grieve is normal, and acknowledging this truth can provide comfort amidst the chaos. Revisiting supportive philosophies or leaning on simple, practical actions can offer a sense of stability as we navigate this messy, unpredictable journey.

Finding Meaning in Loss

Grief reshapes the way we see the world, often pulling us into deep reflection. In the face of loss, people sometimes offer well-meaning but deeply insensitive platitudes—*"everything happens for a reason,"* or *"there must be some meaning in this."* But loss is not a puzzle to solve, nor does it demand that we find meaning as if grief were a lesson we were supposed to learn. Instead, grief invites us to cherish treasured moments and honour the lives of those we have lost.

Memory becomes a cornerstone of this process. By holding onto the small, precious moments we shared—a funny habit, the way they laughed, or the wisdom they imparted—we keep their presence alive. Reflecting on their values and the lessons they left behind can inspire us to carry forward their legacy in our own unique way.

In my own experience, community and friendships became essential. During some of my loneliest days, a wise lady in the village gently reminded me to "stay still," a piece of wisdom that stayed with me, reminding me not to make decisions in haste. Friends would drop by unannounced, offering quiet company when words felt too heavy. And very movingly, someone took down my Christmas decorations—the last ones my husband and I had put up together—when I couldn't bear to face the task myself. These moments, small yet profound, reminded me that even in the deepest throes of loss, we are not truly alone.

I also learned to find comfort and meaning in small, personal rituals. Going to my husband's favourite restaurant and ordering his favourite curry with lime pickle made me feel connected to him, even in his absence. On days when the grief became overwhelming, I would put on his coat, as if wrapping myself in his presence. These simple acts became quiet anchors in my life, offering solace and connection in a way that words never could.

Resilience and growth often emerge when we least expect them. While I would never wish anyone to endure the pain of profound loss, I've come to realise that such experiences can reveal unexpected strength and clarity. They force us to confront life in a new way, helping us find purpose in the aftermath. This isn't to say that loss is ever something we would choose, but rather that the human spirit is remarkably capable of adapting and finding light, even in life's darkest moments.

The interplay of joy and sorrow is another truth I've come to embrace. There were moments of laughter amidst the tears—fleeting but profound reminders of life's duality. While these moments didn't lessen my grief, they showed me that love and loss are intricately connected.

"Light griefs are loquacious, but the great ones are silent" (*Letters to Lucilius*, 63.4).

This quote suggests that smaller troubles or sorrows are often expressed openly and talked about, while deep, profound grief tends to be silent and inexpressible.

To me, it speaks to the nature of intense pain—when we experience minor difficulties, we may vent, complain, or seek comfort in conversation. But when we endure profound loss or suffering, words often fail us. The weight of true grief can be so overwhelming that it leaves us speechless, as if no words could ever capture the depth of our emotions.

It also reflects how people process pain differently—some talk to cope, while others withdraw into silence, bearing the burden within. The quote resonates with the idea that the deepest emotions are often the hardest to articulate.

It reminds us that the deepest pain often exists beyond words, yet it is in these quiet spaces that we can find meaning—not by forcing ourselves to seek it, but by allowing it to emerge naturally over time.

Complicated Relationships and Grief

Grief can become even more complex when the relationship with the deceased was strained or marked by unresolved conflict. In such cases, we may grapple not only with sadness but also with regret, guilt, or anger. The absence of closure can leave us with unanswered questions and the weight of what might have been. These emotions can amplify the grieving process, creating a unique burden that is difficult to navigate.

To cope with these complicated feelings, it may help to focus on radical acceptance—acknowledging the reality of the relationship as it was, rather than as we wish it had been. Finding ways to forgive both ourselves and the deceased for perceived shortcomings can also be healing. Reflecting on the positive aspects of the relationship, no matter how small, may provide some solace. And when resolution feels impossible, allowing ourselves to grieve for the relationship that never was can be an important step in healing.

The Administrative Realities of Loss

Amid the emotional turbulence of grief, we are often confronted with the cold, unyielding reality of administrative tasks. These include sorting out wills, managing estates, planning funerals, and navigating legal procedures—tasks that can feel unbearable when all we want to do is grieve. Yet, they are necessary steps, requiring focus and resolve during one of life's most vulnerable times.

In some cases, these administrative realities can give rise to painful conflicts among family and loved ones. Issues of entitlement, disagreements over wills, or disputes about decisions can erupt, adding an additional layer of distress. When emotions are already raw, it can be difficult to untangle the motives behind others' actions.

Sometimes, what appears to be greed or insensitivity may stem from financial worries or personal struggles that aren't immediately visible. In other cases, it may be a reflection of a deeper personality flaw or unresolved family dynamics. Taking the time to explore what might be driving such behaviour—whether through direct conversation or quiet reflection—can help us decide how to respond.

This process isn't easy, but it can bring clarity. It might reveal an opportunity to extend support and rebuild trust, or it might confirm that setting boundaries or even cutting ties is the healthiest choice. Either way, striving for understanding can guide us towards decisions that honour both the memory of our loved one and our own well-being.

As Jean-Jacques Rousseau wisely observed, "What wisdom can you find that is greater than kindness?" A poignant reminder to approach even the most challenging family conflicts with compassion whenever possible.

Forgiveness, Compassion, and Letting Go of Anger

The death of someone at the hands of another person adds another layer of complexity to grief. When someone is killed, it can awaken a range of emotions, including anger, bitterness, and an overwhelming sense of injustice. This kind of grief often involves navigating legal proceedings, facing the person responsible, or reconciling with the fact that their actions irrevocably altered your life. In such moments, the concept of radical acceptance can be a powerful tool. Radical acceptance does not mean condoning the actions or resigning to injustice; instead, it is about acknowledging the reality of what has happened without resistance. As Tara Brach describes, "Radical acceptance is the willingness to experience our life as it is" (*Radical Acceptance*, 2003). For many, healing comes not from external justice but from finding a way to release the grip of anger, embrace this acceptance, and focus on rebuilding their own lives.

Compassion can also play a role in this process, though it is deeply personal and depends on the circumstances. In some cases, where genuine remorse is shown or accountability is taken, compassion can help to soften the edges of anger and open the door to healing. In others, when no remorse is evident, offering compassion may not feel possible—and that, too, is valid.

What remains essential is extending compassion to ourselves as we navigate grief. It involves acknowledging our pain without judgment and recognising the shared human experience of imperfection and suffering. As the Dalai Lama says, "Compassion is not a luxury; it is a necessity for our well-being, resilience, and survival."

By showing compassion to ourselves, we can begin to ease the emotional burden and create space for healing. This means recognising that our pain is valid and treating ourselves with kindness, even when grief feels overwhelming. Self-compassion allows us to grieve in our own unique way, without judgment, and gives us the strength to rebuild our emotional well-being, one small step at a time.

Living Through Grief: Pain, Suffering, and Renewal

Grief brings with it a brutal reality: at some stage, the lives of those around you begin to return to normal, while yours may not. The funeral arrangements, gatherings, and initial support can feel all-encompassing

Yet, this often gives way to the stark and lonely reality of the day after, which can feel like the loneliest day of your life. Suddenly, reality hits: you are alone. In the weeks that follow, this loneliness can become unbearable, especially if the death was sudden as there was no time to prepare for their departure.

It is at this point that suffering can truly set in, and here the Stoics remind us of a vital truth: the distinction between pain and suffering.

As Seneca wrote, "We often amplify our suffering by imagining scenarios that may never happen" *(*Seneca, Letters to Lucilius, *13.4)*.

Pain is a natural and unavoidable response to loss, but suffering can arise from the narratives we create about that pain. It manifests in thoughts such as wondering what might happen to us now, feeling that life has lost its meaning, or fearing that we will never find happiness again.

These fears, while deeply human, can intensify our suffering and make the road to healing feel insurmountable.

Grief can be overwhelming, often pulling us into cycles of *what-ifs* and imagined scenarios that deepen our suffering. Stoicism reminds us that while pain is inevitable, suffering often arises from resisting reality—wishing things were different or clinging to what we cannot change. Instead, the Stoics encourage us to accept reality as it is and to direct our energy toward what can be changed.

This may feel counterintuitive, but it is vital. Acknowledging the difference between pain and suffering does not diminish the significance of loss but reframes it as a process that, while profoundly difficult, may lead to moments of resilience and renewal.

To rebuild after loss is to embrace the Stoic idea of finding meaning and purpose despite hardship. Rebuilding does not deny grief; rather, it channels it into purposeful actions that acknowledge both the weight of our loss and the strength required to keep moving forward. As Epictetus wisely observed, "Difficulties are things that show a person what they are" (Discourses, *1.24*).

In choosing to rebuild, we honour the memory of our loved ones by living fully and intentionally. This might mean finding new interests, nurturing relationships, or continuing the work they cared about. By doing so, we find moments of strength within grief, easing the grip of suffering and gradually moving toward a life imbued with meaning and purpose.

This is an incredibly difficult step. You will try things that don't work, as I did, but with persistence, you may find something that helps, even if only for a moment. The worst thing I found was to lock myself away. Even small efforts—like reaching out to others, getting up, getting dressed, or calling a friend—made a difference.

As time passed, the natural ebb of support left the house feeling unbearably quiet, reminding me of the importance of connection. Even the smallest actions helped: opening a window, playing music, speaking to someone who understood. These seemingly insignificant steps accumulate over time, creating a foundation for renewal.

I felt it was important to honour the taking of my husband's life by ensuring that mine was not lost to bitterness and despair. The journey has been long and challenging, filled with setbacks and small victories. Writing this book became part of that process—a way to reflect, to heal, and to honour my husband's memory.

I do not want to imply it was easy; every step required effort, and there were days when progress felt impossible. But little by little, through persistence and intention, I found a way forward.

Progress often felt like two steps forward, one step back, but over time, even those small steps began to lead somewhere meaningful.

By choosing to live fully, we do not diminish our grief, but we allow it to transform us, to remind us of the love that shaped us, and to give us the strength to carry it forward.

Friendships and Their Strain During Grief

Grief often places a unique strain on friendships, revealing dynamics that might have otherwise gone unnoticed. Some friends may feel uncomfortable with the intensity of emotions and choose to avoid you, unsure of what to say or how to support you. Others might overcompensate by trying to take control, unintentionally adding stress when all you want is space to grieve.

For couples, your new status as a single person can sometimes feel threatening, leading to distancing behaviours or strained interactions. At times, boundaries can be overlooked, with some individuals misinterpreting your vulnerability or assuming availability for relationships or attention that you may not seek. These experiences create an emotional rollercoaster, further complicating an already challenging time.

Navigating these strains requires both patience and clarity. Communicating your needs—whether for space, understanding, or support—can help preserve important friendships while letting go of those that no longer serve your well-being. Grief is a deeply personal journey and surrounding yourself with those who respect your boundaries and offer unconditional support is essential for healing.

As Epictetus teaches, "The key is to keep company only with people who uplift you, whose presence calls forth your best" (*Discourses*, 3.16).

This wisdom reminds us that not all friendships withstand the weight of grief, and that's okay. Allowing relationships to shift, or even to end, is part of honouring your healing process.

Judgment When Meeting Someone New

As we begin to heal and consider moving forward, meeting someone new can often invite judgment from others. Friends, family, and even acquaintances may feel compelled to weigh in with their opinions—whether on how soon is "too soon" or whether moving forward is appropriate at all. This scrutiny often stems from misconceptions about grief, such as the mistaken belief that finding happiness again somehow diminishes the memory of a lost loved one. In some cases, this judgment reflects others' discomfort with change or their projection of personal expectations onto your choices.

While such reactions can be hurtful, it's important to remember that grief is an intensely personal journey. Seeking companionship or love does not erase the significance of what was lost. Instead, it can mark the beginning of a new chapter—one where the memory of your loved one remains with you, even as you open yourself to the possibility of connection and joy once more.

Navigating this path requires self-compassion and clear boundaries. Trust yourself to know what feels right. Focus on your own journey rather than being swayed by external voices or timelines. Grief does not follow a universal pattern, and neither does the rediscovery of happiness. Healing is not about meeting others' expectations. Allow yourself the grace to embrace healing in your own way and at your own pace.

A Final Note

Grief changes us in ways we never anticipated. It reminds us of the depth of our love and the reality of loss. It's not a lesson we seek but one we endure, learning what it means to adapt and keep moving forward in the wake of profound pain.

In the overwhelming moments, it's okay to feel lost. Healing isn't linear, and some days will feel heavier than others. Taking small steps, even when they seem insignificant—like getting dressed or stepping outside—can be acts of strength. Rest when you need to, and allow yourself the time and space to find your way, even if that way looks different than you imagined.

As Seneca wisely wrote, "Time discovers truth. Time heals what reason cannot" (*Letters to Lucilius*, 78.23).

Let time do its work. Grief will never fully leave you, but neither will love. And in that, there is a quiet, enduring strength.

7

EMBRACING LIFE BY FACING DEATH

THE WISDOM OF MEMENTO MORI

"It is not death that a man should fear, but he should fear never beginning to live."

— MARCUS AURELIUS, *MEDITATIONS*

FEW TOPICS FEEL as universal yet avoided as death. Across the globe, over 170,000 people pass away each day (World Health Organization, 2020). Yet how often do we truly confront the inevitability of our own mortality? Instead, we bury it beneath the busyness of life, distracted by the mundane. The irony is this: we fear death most when we're not fully living. By failing to engage deeply with life, death becomes the thief lurking in the shadows. But what if death could instead be a guide—a reminder to live with clarity and intention?

This chapter explores how facing death head-on can transform the way we live. Through the wisdom of ancient philosophy, modern psychology, and diverse cultural practices, we can learn how mortality, far from being a source of despair, holds the key to a life well-lived.

What Do We Truly Fear? The Untapped Power of Mortality

On their deathbeds, people rarely fear death itself. What haunts them most are regrets—the words left unsaid, the dreams abandoned, the life they postponed for "someday." This idea is echoed by Bronnie Ware, a palliative care nurse whose book, *The Top Five Regrets of the Dying* (2012), reveals that the most common regret is not having had the courage to live true to oneself, instead of conforming to the expectations of others. In many ways, it is not death we fear, but an unlived life.

Yet, if we allow it, the awareness of mortality can be a source of liberation rather than fear. Instead of trapping us in anxiety, it can shift our focus to the present, urging us to fully embrace life while we can.

"Do not act as if you were going to live ten thousand years. Death hangs over you. While you live, while it is in your power, be good" (Aurelius, trans. Hays, 2002).

For Aurelius, the true danger was not death itself but living without purpose. Similarly, Seneca warns against the illusion of unlimited time:

"Let us postpone nothing. Let us balance life's books every day. The one who puts the finishing touches on their life each day is never short of time" (*Letters to Lucilius*, trans. Campbell, 1969).

This is not an argument for rushing through life, but rather for living with intention. Every moment spent fearing death is a moment stolen from life.

This understanding is not unique to Stoicism. In Tibetan Buddhism, the practice of *Lojong*—meditating on impermanence and death—serves as a powerful reminder to embrace life's fleeting nature rather than resist it (Trungpa, 1973). Far from being morbid, this practice fosters compassion and clarity, helping individuals to live more fully in the present.

Stephen Hawking embodied this same philosophy in a modern context. Diagnosed with a terminal illness at a young age, he transformed the awareness of his mortality into a force for achievement. Instead of wasting time fearing the inevitable, he dedicated his life to knowledge and inspiration, leaving an extraordinary legacy (Ferguson, 2011).

Mortality, then, is not something to be feared, but a call to awareness. It is not a shadow over our existence, but a call to live with urgency, purpose, and gratitude.

The Psychology of Mortality: Why Fear Can Be a Catalyst

Modern psychology sheds light on how the awareness of death can shape our behaviour in profound ways. For instance, imagine a person suddenly reminded of their mortality through the loss of a loved one or a personal health scare. This moment often sparks reflection: Am I spending my time on what truly matters?

Terror Management Theory (TMT), developed by Greenberg, Pyszczynski, and Solomon (1986), reveals that confronting our mortality can inspire us to seek meaning and align our lives with our deepest values. Research by Pyszczynski et al. (2004) demonstrated that participants reminded of their mortality were more likely to engage in prosocial behaviours, such as donating to charity or expressing greater compassion.

A study published in the *Journal of Experimental Social Psychology* found that individuals who reflected on their mortality reported heightened gratitude and prioritized meaningful experiences over trivial distractions (Routledge & Juhl, 2011). This highlights how such reflections can lead to a deeper appreciation for the present, encouraging a more intentional way of living. In one scenario from the study, participants reported being more likely to savour small, daily joys, such as conversations with loved ones or moments in nature, underscoring the transformative potential of confronting death.

But the opposite is also true. When we repress thoughts of death, we tend to numb ourselves with distractions—endless scrolling, overwork, or shallow pursuits. These coping mechanisms leave us more disconnected from life, intensifying the very fear we're trying to escape.

Cultural Wisdom: Lessons on Living from Around the World

Across cultures, people have found ways to embrace mortality as a source of meaning. In Mexico, the Day of the Dead (Día de los Muertos) reframes death as a celebration of life. Families honour their ancestors by creating colourful altars, sharing stories, and gathering for communal remembrance (Brandes, 1998). This tradition is a vivid reminder that death is not separate from life, but a continuation of it.

In Japan, the cherry blossom (sakura) symbolises the beauty of impermanence. The fleeting bloom of these delicate flowers inspires people to cherish transient moments (Inaga, 2005). Similarly, Tibetan sky burials treat death as a natural cycle, returning the body to the earth to nourish other beings. These practices reflect an understanding that death, rather than being feared, can be a profound reminder of life's interconnectedness and value.

Even Western cultures are rediscovering the value of facing mortality. For instance, the emergence of death cafes and end-of-life planning workshops provides modern spaces to engage with mortality openly and honestly. These settings encourage conversations that, while often difficult, lead to deeper clarity about priorities and values. Such practices echo ancient wisdom by showing that, by confronting death, we can better understand life and its inherent preciousness.

The Mystery of Sensing Death

One of the more enigmatic aspects of mortality is the question of whether we can sense our own death approaching. While empirical evidence to confirm this phenomenon remains limited, anecdotal accounts abound. Some survivors of near-death experiences report an eerie sense of forewarning—a gut feeling or moment of inexplicable clarity in the hours or minutes before an accident or crisis (Moody, 1975).

For those left behind, like the families of those who pass

suddenly, this question often lingers: *Did they sense it? Were they afraid?* While research into precognition of death is speculative, studies on end-of-life awareness suggest that some individuals, particularly the terminally ill, often speak of impending death in symbolic ways before passing (Fenwick et al., 2009).

Fear of the pain of dying also weighs heavily on many minds. The unknown—whether it will hurt, whether suffering will be involved—creates a deeply human anxiety. Yet, in moments of reflection, it becomes clear that this fear, too, can be eased by the way we live.

Living with intention and clarity can help us meet death's approach with readiness rather than panic. As Stephen Levine wrote in *A Year to Live*, "If we truly face the fact that we are going to die, we stop pretending and begin to live with an open heart" (Levine, 1997, p. 22).

Do We Fear the Aftermath or Its Absence?

Our attitudes toward death often depend on whether we believe in an existence beyond it. For some, faith in an afterlife—whether spiritual or religious—brings comfort and a sense of continuity, alleviating the fear of finality (Becker, 1973). Others, however, see death as a definitive end, a cessation of consciousness.

For those who hold the latter belief, the absence of an afterlife creates a heightened pressure to make life count. Without the promise of eternity, the stakes for living meaningfully in the present become more urgent (Nagel, 1979).

Psychological research supports this divide. A 2017 study in Death Studies by Jong and Halberstadt found that individuals with strong beliefs in an afterlife exhibited lower levels of death anxiety and were more at peace with their impermanence (Jong & Halberstadt, 2017). On the other hand, those who did not believe in an afterlife reported greater urgency to achieve personal goals and leave a legacy, as they viewed their impact as confined to this lifetime.

Regardless of belief, reflecting on death—and its potential aftermath or lack thereof—offers clarity. It challenges us to ask:

- Are we living authentically, in alignment with our values?
- Are we focused on what truly matters?

As the Stoics remind us, fearing death is less about death itself and more about not having lived well. The only way to ease the fear of death is to make peace with life—to live with intention, courage, and virtue so that when the time comes, we do not meet it with regret but with acceptance.

The Duty to Leave Things in Order: Practical Wisdom

A lesser discussed but deeply meaningful aspect of embracing mortality is the responsibility to leave our affairs in order. This extends beyond personal possessions to ensuring clarity for those left behind.

It's vital to have a will in place and to make final wishes clear. This includes not only how pets should be cared for and how possessions should be distributed but also specifying funeral arrangements. When left unaddressed, these uncertainties often place significant emotional and financial burdens on loved ones (Callanan & Kelley, 1997). Conversations about payment for services, burial or cremation preferences, and the tone of any ceremonies should not be avoided, even though they may feel uncomfortable.

For those facing terminal illnesses such as cancer or dementia, preparing a living will and appointing a power of attorney (POA) is crucial. A living will outlines preferences for medical treatment if one becomes unable to communicate, while a POA ensures that someone trusted can make critical decisions on one's behalf. These steps preserve autonomy while alleviating stress on family members during critical moments (Singer et al., 1999).

The Swedish concept of "*döstädning,*" or "death cleaning,"

encourages individuals to declutter their lives and simplify possessions—not just for their own peace of mind, but to relieve the emotional and logistical burden on loved ones (Magnusson, 2018). This act of preparation can be both practical and symbolic, a way of taking control of one's legacy.

However, death cleaning doesn't mean stripping life of joy. Rather, it's about prioritizing what truly matters—cherished memories, meaningful possessions, and clarity for those who remain. Organizing financial documents and even leaving behind personal notes or messages are acts of love that ensure one's departure does not create unnecessary chaos.

Preparing for death in this way also prompts reflection on life. As Margareta Magnusson, author of *The Gentle Art of Swedish Death Cleaning*, suggests: "Life will become more pleasant and comfortable if we get rid of some of the abundance" (Magnusson, 2018, p. 34).

By clearing the unnecessary, we make space for deeper connection and intentional living.

Embracing Mortality: From Fear to Freedom

When we accept death, we reclaim our power. Nelson Mandela's 27 years of imprisonment under the threat of death didn't break him; it liberated him. By accepting his mortality, he freed himself from fear and focused on what truly mattered: his vision for a free South Africa. As he later said: "I learned that courage was not the absence of fear, but the triumph over it" (Mandela, 1994, p. 115).

Similarly, Admiral James Stockdale, who survived years as a prisoner of war, maintained his resilience by focusing only on what was within his control. Accepting the possibility of death allowed him to preserve his integrity, discipline, and mental strength (Stockdale, 1993).

When we stop running from mortality, we free ourselves from the trivialities that often dominate life. The petty arguments, the relentless pursuit of status, the fear of failure—these lose their grip when we recognize the finite nature of time.

Living with Intention: Practices for a Meaningful Life

How can we use the awareness of death to live more fully? Here are three practices inspired by ancient wisdom and cultural traditions:

1. **Practice** *Memento Mori* - Carry a reminder of mortality —a coin, bracelet, or journal entry. Reflect on impermanence daily, not to dwell on fear, but to ground yourself in what truly matters. Let this guide you toward meaningful relationships and experiences (Holiday, 2016).
2. **Focus on What You Can Control** - Seneca's advice resonates here: "He who fears death will never do anything worth a man who is alive" (Seneca, trans. Campbell, 1969). Instead of wasting energy worrying about how much time remains, ask: Are my actions aligned with my values? Am I living authentically?
3. **Create Your Legacy** - What do you wish to leave behind? Whether nurturing relationships, creating art, or serving your community, your contributions give your life enduring meaning. Legacy isn't about fame—it's about impact.

Interactive Reflection: Designing a Life Worth Living

To deepen engagement with these ideas, try these reflection exercises:

1. ***One-Year Timeline:*** If you had one year to live, how would you spend it? What would you change about your relationships, career, or daily routines?
2. ***Life's End Reflection:*** Imagine yourself at the end of your life. What do you want to be remembered for? How can your current actions reflect this vision?

3. ***Savour Small Joys:*** Identify one small joy you often overlook. How can you fully appreciate it today?

A Final Thought

Death isn't the enemy; it's a mirror. It reflects the urgency to live fully and intentionally. By embracing mortality, we strip away distractions—status, material gain, petty concerns—and centre ourselves on what truly matters: love, purpose, and presence.

As Marcus Aurelius reminds us: "You could leave life right now. Let that determine what you do and say and think" (Aurelius, trans. Hays, 2002).

8

ANCHORED IN CHAOS

A STOIC APPROACH TO LIVING WITH INTENTION

As I reflect on the journey that led me to write this book, I am reminded of one central truth: everything is interconnected. From the smallest moment of introspection to the vast, unfolding fabric of the universe, our lives are a dance of connection and influence. When we truly grasp this interconnection, we unlock the transformative power of the mind to shape both our own experiences and the world around us.

Stoicism teaches us that while we cannot control external events, we can master our internal world—our thoughts, our choices, our reactions. Marcus Aurelius wrote, "All things are woven together, and the common bond is sacred... for they have been arranged together in their proper places and compose one orderly universe" (Aurelius, trans. 2002, p. 74).

When life challenges us with loss, uncertainty, or hardship, our natural instinct might be to retreat or resist. Yet, the Stoics remind us that these moments are opportunities for growth and transformation. By focusing on what is within our control, we can find clarity and resilience amid the chaos.

The Power of Presence

Seneca wrote, "We are tormented alike by what is past and what is to come. But a man who has learned how to live for the present day alone, has attained eternity" (Seneca, trans. 1997, p. 102).

The past cannot be rewritten, and the future remains uncertain. The only time we truly have is now. This understanding is more than philosophical—it is profoundly practical. It reminds us to show up fully in our relationships, to embrace joy where we find it, and to meet each moment with intention.

Marcus Aurelius offers another essential perspective. "What injures the hive, injures the bee" (Aurelius, trans. 2002, p. 85).

When we focus only on our individual struggles or desires, we forget that our well-being is intertwined with that of others. Just as each bee contributes to the survival of the hive, our choices ripple outward, shaping not only our personal lives but the broader communities we are part of. Living with presence, care, and integrity strengthens the entire web of existence.

Modern science echoes this idea. The principle of quantum entanglement reveals that two particles, once connected, remain linked across vast distances. This serves as a powerful metaphor for human existence: every thought, every action sends ripples through the interconnected web of reality. By shifting our perspective and choosing intention over reactivity, we not only adapt to the world—we help shape it.

Resilience Through Loss

This understanding has been both a comfort and a guide in my own life. When I faced the sudden death of my husband, I was forced to confront the fragility and interconnectedness of existence. Grief, I discovered, is not something to be conquered but integrated. It illuminates what truly matters: the preciousness of time, the importance of presence, and the courage to remain open to life's uncertainties.

In those darkest days, the Stoic principle of focusing on what was within my control became a lifeline. I could not bring my husband back, nor could I undo the pain of his absence. But I could choose how to live in the wake of that loss. I could either become bitter and allow grief to diminish me, or I could honour his memory by embracing life with greater intention and gratitude. Each choice became a thread in the tapestry of a new reality—one woven not out of despair but resilience.

Be Gentle with Yourself

Stoicism is often perceived as rigid or unemotional, but at its core, it is a deeply compassionate philosophy. It reminds us that mastery is not perfection, and wisdom is not achieved overnight. As Marcus Aurelius reassures us, "When you arise in the morning, think of what a privilege it is to be alive—to breathe, to think, to enjoy, to love" (Aurelius, trans. 2002, p. 58).

This is not about being unshaken by life's hardships but about continually returning to our practice. The journey toward resilience, peace, and self-mastery is not linear. There will be moments of struggle, but each time we come back to these principles, we strengthen the foundation upon which our lives are built.

Regret as a Teacher

One of my biggest regrets is not thinking things through as deeply as I could have at pivotal moments in my life. In hindsight, I see how impulsive choices or unexamined decisions contributed to unnecessary difficulties. The Stoics, however, teach us to approach regret not as a source of self-recrimination but as a guide for future growth.

Seneca wrote, "It is not that we have a short time to live, but that we waste much of it" (Seneca, trans. 1997, p. 14).

This reminds us that thoughtlessness often stems from a failure to appreciate the value of time and deliberate action. One way to avoid future regret is through *Premeditatio Malorum*, the

Stoic practice of envisioning possible difficulties in advance. By mentally preparing for challenges before they arise, we can respond with clarity rather than impulsivity. Instead of reacting to life's events with hindsight, we learn to meet them with foresight.

Regret is not a life sentence—it is an invitation to act with greater purpose and thoughtfulness in the present.

A Call to Action: Living with Intention

So, what does this mean for you, the reader? It means recognizing that you are not a passive observer of your life but an active participant. The principles of Stoicism—accepting what you cannot control, focusing on what you can, and cultivating inner strength—are tools for transforming your perspective. When combined with an understanding of interconnection, they reveal a deeper truth: the power to reshape your world begins within.

Living with intention means making deliberate choices rather than drifting through life on autopilot. It means pausing before reacting, asking whether your actions align with your values, and choosing responses that reflect wisdom rather than impulse. It is about bringing awareness to the present moment and ensuring that your daily habits, decisions, and interactions reflect the person you aspire to be.

But this is not about rigid control or perfection. Living with intention also requires flexibility—the ability to adapt, to accept setbacks with grace, and to recognize that growth is an ongoing process. The Stoics remind us that life will always present challenges, but it is our response to them that defines us.

Every thought you nurture, every action you take, contributes to the larger whole. Your choices matter. By choosing intention, by aligning your thoughts and actions with purpose, you can create ripples of positive change that extend far beyond yourself. You are part of a grander pattern, one that is constantly evolving and offering opportunities for growth and transformation.

As you move forward, consider this: what kind of impact do you want to create in the world? How can you align your inner strength with the interconnected web of existence? The answers may not come all at once, and that is fine. It begins with small steps: cultivating gratitude, letting go of what you cannot control, and embracing the present moment with courage and clarity.

The chaos of life will not disappear, but your relationship with it can transform. Through the power of your mind, your choices, and your connection to the greater whole, you can live not just reactively but intentionally. This is the essence of freedom and the path to a life of meaning and purpose.

Thank you for joining me on this journey. May you find strength in the interconnections that bind us all, and may you embrace the courage to shape your world with intention and grace.

AUTHOR'S NOTE

Referencing the Nine Core Principles

These principles are not a strict list found in any single Stoic text. Marcus Aurelius never laid them out in a numbered format—instead, they are recurring ideas woven throughout his *Meditations* and the teachings of Epictetus and Seneca.

For that reason, you may see them worded slightly differently in various translations or interpretations. The core ideas remain the same, but different writers, translators, and scholars may emphasise them in their own way.

Rather than being a fixed doctrine, these principles bring together key Stoic ideas in a way that makes them easier to apply in daily life. They provide a practical framework for living with virtue, control, and action—the essential ingredients of Stoic self-discipline.

Disclaimer: This reference guide is an independent interpretation of Stoic themes and is not affiliated with or endorsed by any specific translation or publisher. Citations from *Meditations* are provided for ease of reference and may include widely available translations, such as the Penguin Classics edition translated by Martin Hammond (2006 Reference Guide: *Mapping* *the Nine Core Stoic Principles to Meditations* (Penguin Classics, Martin Hammond Translation, 2006).

Overview

The *Penguin Classics* edition of *Meditations* by Marcus Aurelius does not explicitly list "The Nine Core Stoic Principles" as a structured framework. However, the key Stoic ideas that form the foundation of these principles are present throughout the text. The Nine Core Beliefs are a modern synthesis of recurring Stoic themes rather than something Marcus Aurelius explicitly laid out in a numbered format.

This guide serves as a quick reference for readers, helping them connect modern Stoic practice to its ancient roots within *Meditations*.

How the Nine Core Stoic Principles Align with *Meditations*

The Dichotomy of Control, Virtue as the Highest Good, Memento Mori, Amor Fati, and the other principles are all supported by passages from *Meditations*.

The specific book and section numbers from Martin Hammond's translation (2006) match each principle in this reference.

The modern framework (Nine Core Beliefs) is a structured extraction of Marcus Aurelius' discussions on Stoicism throughout *Meditations*.

This reference guide serves as a quick-access tool to help readers find direct links between modern Stoic practice and its classical foundations. By studying these passages, readers can deepen their understanding of how Marcus Aurelius embodied these principles in his own life and how they remain applicable today.

If you wish to explore Stoicism further, refer to *Meditations* in the Penguin Classics edition (translated by Martin Hammond, 2006) for a deeper connection to these timeless teachings.

Mapping the Nine Core Stoic Principles to *Meditations*

Stoic Principle	Key Passages in *Meditations*	Marcus Aurelius' Key Ideas
1. The Dichotomy of Control	Book 5, Section 20Book 6, Section 41Book 8, Section 7Book 12, Section 22	"You have power over your mind—not outside events. Realize this, and you will find strength." Focus on controlling your mind, actions, and responses, not external events.
2. Virtue is the Highest Good (Summum Bonum)	Book 3, Section 6Book 6, Section 16Book 6, Section 30Book 7, Section 15	"If, at some point in life, you should come across anything better than justice, truth, self-control, and courage, it must be an extraordinary thing indeed." Virtue (Wisdom, Courage, Justice, Temperance) is the only real good.
3. Memento Mori (Remembering Mortality)	Book 2, Section 11Book 4, Section 17Book 6, Section 47Book 7, Section 69	"You could leave life right now. Let that determine what you do and say and think." Reflecting on death brings urgency to life and keeps priorities clear.
4. Amor Fati (Loving and Accepting Fate)	Book 4, Section 26Book 5, Section 8Book 10, Section 5Book 10, Section 8	"Everything that happens, happens as it should, and if you observe carefully, you will find this to be so." Embrace fate instead of resisting it. See obstacles as part of nature's plan.
5. Negative Visualisation (Premeditatio Malorum)	Book 9, Section 21Book 12, Section 26Book 4, Section 49	"Expect to face criticism, betrayal, and hardship—this is the nature of human life. When it comes, you will not be surprised." Prepare for difficulties mentally, so you remain steady when they arrive.
6. The View from Above	Book 5, Section 24Book 7, Section 47Book 9, Section 32	"Look at the vastness of the universe, and your troubles will seem small." Step back and see life from a higher perspective to reduce stress and personal ego.

Stoic Principle	Key Passages in *Meditations*	Marcus Aurelius' Key Ideas
7. Sympatheia (Shared Humanity & Connection)	Book 2, Section 1Book 6, Section 39Book 9, Section 9Book 11, Section 8	"We are all made for cooperation, like feet, hands, and eyelids." We are part of a greater whole and should act with justice and empathy.
8. Discipline & Temperance	Book 7, Section 31Book 8, Section 51Book 10, Section 37Book 12, Section 19	"Don't waste time arguing what a good person should be. Be one." Master desires, impulses, and actions through self-discipline.
9. Continual Self-Improvement (Progress, Not Perfection)	Book 4, Section 12Book 5, Section 9Book 6, Section 30Book 8, Section 7	"Be tolerant with others and strict with yourself." Life is a process of constant growth. Keep improving.

Key Takeaways

- *Meditations* does not explicitly list these as "The Nine Core Beliefs," but Marcus Aurelius touches on all of them throughout the book.
- These principles are extracted from various Stoic writings (including Epictetus & Seneca) and organised into a modern framework for easier application.
- This table provides direct references to the Martin Hammond translation, making it easier for readers to locate passages supporting each principle.

ABOUT THE AUTHOR

Emily's life has been anything but predictable, full of unexpected twists—some challenging, some rewarding. Having spent the past few years living abroad, she often reflects on how our perspectives shape our experiences. She's drawn to the idea that while we can't always control what happens, we can choose how we respond.

Her book is inspired by her grandma, a strong and pragmatic woman whose words—*"It is, and that's an end of it; now what are you going to do?"*—capture the essence of resilience and acceptance. These ideas shape Emily's own view of life: while uncertainty is inevitable, we have the power to navigate it with purpose. Through her writing, she explores the relationship between choice, perception, and the way we move forward, inviting readers to approach life's uncertainties with curiosity and determination.

BIBLIOGRAPHY

Aurelius, M. (2002). Meditations (G. Hays, Trans.). Modern Library.

Aurelius, M. (2006). Meditations (M. Hammond, Trans.). Penguin Classics. (Original work published c. 180)

Beck, A. T. (1976). Cognitive therapy and the emotional disorders. International Universities Press.

Bianchi, S. M. (2011). Changing rhythms of American family life. Russell Sage Foundation.

Brach, T. (2003). Radical Acceptance: Embracing Your Life with the Heart of a Buddha. Bantam.

Brandes, S. (1998). Iconography in Mexico's Day of the Dead: Origins and meaning. Ethnohistory, 45(2), 181-218.

Brown, B. (2018). Dare to lead: Brave work. Tough conversations. Whole hearts. Random House.

Brown, B. B., & Larson, R. W. (2009). Peer relationships in adolescence. In R. M. Lerner & L. Steinberg (Eds.), Handbook of adolescent psychology (3rd ed., Vol. 2, pp. 74-103). Wiley.

Brynjolfsson, E., Horton, J. J., Ozimek, A., Rock, D., Sharma, G., & TuYe, H.-Y. (2020). COVID-19 and remote work: An early look at trends and implications. National Bureau of Economic Research.

Callanan, M., & Kelley, P. (1997). Final gifts: Understanding the special awareness, needs, and communications of the dying. Simon & Schuster.

Cuevas, B. (2007). The Hidden History of Tibetan Sky Burial. Columbia University Press.

Dalai Lama. (Various works).

Diogenes Laërtius. (1925). Lives of eminent philosophers (R. D. Hicks, Trans.). Harvard University Press.

Dispenza, J. (2017). Becoming supernatural: How common people are doing the uncommon. Hay House.

Durvasula, R. (2019). Don't you know who I am? How to stay sane in an era of narcissism, entitlement, and incivility. Post Hill Press.

Ellis, A. (1962). Reason and emotion in psychotherapy. Lyle Stuart.

Epictetus. (1995). The Discourses of Epictetus (R. Hard, Trans.). Everyman's Library.

Epictetus. (2008). Discourses and selected writings (R. Hard, Trans.). Penguin Classics.

Epictetus. (2008). The Discourses of Epictetus (R. Hard, Trans.). Penguin Classics.

Epictetus. (Discourses). (Various translations available).

Fenwick, P., Lovelace, H., & Brayne, S. (2009). End-of-life experiences: Reaching out for compassion, communication, and connection—meaning at life's end. American Journal of Hospice & Palliative Medicine, 26(2), 103-111.

Ferguson, K. (2011). Stephen Hawking: His Life and Work. Bantam Books.

Festinger, L. (1954). A theory of social comparison processes. Human Relations, 7(2), 117-140. https://doi.org/10.1177/001872675400700202.

Gillis, A. (2023). Stepsibling rivalry and bullying: 11 tips for blended families. Healthline. Retrieved from https://www.healthline.com/health/parenting/step-sibling-rivalry.

Gillis, J. R. (2023). Family roles and psychological adaptation: A longitudinal study. Cambridge University Press.

Grant, A. (2013). Give and take: Why helping others drives our success. Viking.

Greenberg, J., Pyszczynski, T., & Solomon, S. (1986). The causes and consequences of a need for self-esteem: A terror management theory. Psychological Bulletin, 96(3), 650-678.

Hadot, P. (1995). Philosophy as a way of life: Spiritual exercises from Socrates to Foucault (A. Davidson & M. Chase, Trans.). Blackwell.

Hadot, P. (1995). Philosophy as a way of life: Spiritual exercises from Socrates to Foucault. Blackwell.

Haidt, J. (2023). The anxious generation: How the great rewiring of childhood is causing an epidemic of mental illness. Allen Lane.

Holiday, R. (2016). The daily stoic: 366 meditations on wisdom, perseverance, and the art of living. Portfolio.

Holiday, R., & Hanselman, S. (2020). The Daily Stoic: 366 meditations on wisdom, perseverance, and the art of living. Portfolio.

Irvine, W. B. (2008). A guide to the good life: The ancient art of Stoic joy. Oxford University Press.

Jong, J., & Halberstadt, J. (2017). Death anxiety and religious belief: A meta-analysis. Death Studies, 41(8), 491-504.

Kumar, S., et al. (2015). The neuroscience of solitude and its cognitive benefits. Journal of Cognitive Neuroscience.

Kübler-Ross, E. (2005). On grief and grieving: Finding the meaning of grief through the five stages of loss. Scribner.

Lao Tzu. (Tao Te Ching). (Various translations available).

Levine, S. (1997). A year to live: How to live this year as if it were your last. Harmony.

Long, A. A. (2002). Epictetus: A Stoic and Socratic guide to life. Oxford University Press.

Luthar, S. S., Kumar, N. L., & Zillmer, N. (2019). High-achieving parents: Parenting stress and resilience. Psychological Bulletin, 145(5), 437–465. https://doi.org/10.1037/bul0000182.

Magnusson, M. (2018). The gentle art of Swedish death cleaning. Scribner.

Mandela, N. (1994). Long walk to freedom: The autobiography of Nelson Mandela. Little, Brown.

Market Research Future. (2023). Baby care products market analysis.

Minuchin, S. (1974). Families and family therapy. Harvard University Press.

Moody, R. A. (1975). Life after life: The investigation of a phenomenon—survival of bodily death. Bantam.

Newport, C. (2016). Deep work: Rules for focused success in a distracted world. Grand Central Publishing.

Pang, A. (2019). Rest: Why you get more done when you work less. Basic Books.

Papernow, P. L. (2013). Surviving and thriving in stepfamily relationships: What works and what doesn't. Routledge.

Pigliucci, M. (2017). How to be a Stoic: Using ancient philosophy to live a modern life. Basic Books.

PsychCentral. (2023). The science of solitude and mental well-being. Retrieved from www.psychcentral.com.

Robertson, D. (2019). How to think like a Roman emperor: The Stoic philosophy of Marcus Aurelius. St. Martin's Press.

Rousseau, J. J. (Emile, or On Education). (Various translations available).

Seneca. (1917). Moral Letters to Lucilius (R. M. Gummere, Trans.). Harvard University Press.

Seneca. (1997). Letters from a Stoic (R. Campbell, Trans.). Penguin Classics.

Twenge, J. M. (2017). iGen: Why today's super-connected kids are growing up less rebellious, more tolerant, less happy—and completely unprepared for adulthood. Atria Books.

World Health Organization. (2020). Global Health Estimates. Geneva: WHO.

Yousafzai, M., & Lamb, C. (2013). I Am Malala: The Girl Who Stood Up for Education and Was Shot by the Taliban. Little, Brown.

Printed in Great Britain
by Amazon

61450849R10080